The World of the

Ten Thousand Things

Charles Wright

THE WORLD

OF THE

TEN THOUSAND

THINGS

Poems 1980–1990

Farrar, Straus and Giroux

New York

Printed in the United States of America
First published in 1990 by Farrar, Straus and Giroux
First paperback edition, 1991
16   15   14   13   12   11   10   9   8   7   6

Library of Congress catalog card number: 90-71121

Acknowledgments are made to the following publications,
in whose pages some of the poems in Xioma first appeared:
Poetry Magazine, Western Humanities Review, The New
Republic, The Ontario Review, The Paris Review,
Antaeus, *and* The New Yorker.

A fine-press limited edition at Xiomia has been published
by K. K. Merker at the Windhover Press, Iowa City,
Iowa.
Paperback ISBN: 0-374-52326-6

Contents

The Other Side of the River (1984)

Zone Journals (1988)

Xionia (1990)

THE

SOUTHERN

CROSS

(1981)

Homage to Paul Cézanne

At night, in the fish-light of the moon, the dead wear our white shirts
To stay warm, and litter the fields.
We pick them up in the mornings, dewy pieces of paper and scraps of
    cloth.
Like us, they refract themselves. Like us,
They keep on saying the same thing, trying to get it right.
Like us, the water unsettles their names.

Sometimes they lie like leaves in their little arks, and curl up at the
    edges.
Sometimes they come inside, wearing our shoes, and walk
From mirror to mirror.
Or lie in our beds with their gloves off
And touch our bodies. Or talk
In a corner. Or wait like envelopes on a desk.

They reach up from the ice plant.
They shuttle their messengers through the oat grass.
Their answers rise like rust on the stalks and the spidery leaves.

We rub them off our hands.

Each year the dead grow less dead, and nudge
Close to the surface of all things.
They start to remember the silence that brought them there.
They start to recount the gain in their soiled hands.

Their glasses let loose, and grain by grain return to the riverbank.
They point to their favorite words
Growing around them, revealed as themselves for the first time:
They stand close to the meanings and take them in.

They stand there, vague and without pain,
Under their fingernails an unreturnable dirt.
They stand there and it comes back,
The music of everything, syllable after syllable

Out of the burning chair, out of the beings of light.
It all comes back.
And what they repeat to themselves, and what they repeat to
        themselves,
Is the song that our fathers sing.

In steeps and sighs,
The ocean explains itself, backing and filling
What spaces it can't avoid, spaces
In black shoes, their hands clasped, their eyes teared at the edges:
We watch from the high hillside,
The ocean swelling and flattening, the spaces
Filling and emptying, horizon blade
Flashing the early afternoon sun.

The dead are constant in
The white lips of the sea.
Over and over, through clenched teeth, they tell
Their story, the story each knows by heart:
Remember me, speak my name.
When the moon tugs at my sleeve,
When the body of water is raised and becomes the body of light,
Remember me, speak my name.

The dead are a cadmium blue.
We spread them with palette knives in broad blocks and planes.

We layer them stroke by stroke
In steps and ascending mass, in verticals raised from the earth.

We choose, and layer them in,
Blue and a blue and a breath,

Circle and smudge, cross-beak and buttonhook,
We layer them in. We squint hard and terrace them line by line.

And so we are come between, and cry out,
And stare up at the sky and its cloudy panes,

And finger the cypress twists.
The dead understand all this, and keep in touch,

Rustle of hand to hand in the lemon trees,
Flags, and the great sifts of anger

To powder and nothingness.
The dead are a cadmium blue, and they understand.

The dead are with us to stay.
Their shadows rock in the back yard, so pure, so black,
Between the oak tree and the porch.

Over our heads they're huge in the night sky.
In the tall grass they turn with the zodiac.
Under our feet they're white with the snows of a thousand years.

They carry their colored threads and baskets of silk
To mend our clothes, making us look right,
Altering, stitching, replacing a button, closing a tear.
They lie like tucks in our loose sleeves, they hold us together.

They blow the last leaves away.
They slide like an overflow into the river of heaven.
Everywhere they are flying.

The dead are a sleight and a fade
We fall for, like flowering plums, like white coins from the rain.
Their sighs are gaps in the wind.

7)

The dead are waiting for us in our rooms,
Little globules of light
In one of the far corners, and close to the ceiling, hovering, thinking
    our thoughts.

Often they'll reach a hand down,
Or offer a word, and ease us out of our bodies to join them in theirs.
We look back at our other selves on the bed.

We look back and we don't care and we go.

And thus we become what we've longed for,
                                    past tense and otherwise,
A BB, a disc of light,
                    song without words.
And refer to ourselves
In the third person, seeing that other arm
Still raised from the bed, fingers like licks and flames in the boned air.

Only to hear that it's not time.
Only to hear that we must re-enter and lie still, our arms at rest at our
    sides,
The voices rising around us like mist

And dew, *it's all right, it's all right, it's all right* . . .

The dead fall around us like rain.
They come down from the last clouds in the late light for the last time
And slip through the sod.

They lean uphill and face north.
                    Like grass,
They bend toward the sea, they break toward the setting sun.

We filigree and we baste.
But what do the dead care for the fringe of words,
Safe in their suits of milk?
What do they care for the honk and flash of a new style?

And who is to say if the inch of snow in our hearts
Is rectitude enough?

Spring picks the locks of the wind.
High in the night sky the mirror is hauled up and unsheeted.
In it we twist like stars.

Ahead of us, through the dark, the dead
Are beating their drums and stirring the yellow leaves.

We're out here, our feet in the soil, our heads craned up at the sky,
The stars streaming and bursting behind the trees.

At dawn, as the clouds gather, we watch
The mountain glide from the east on the valley floor,
Coming together in starts and jumps.
Behind their curtain, the bears
Amble across the heavens, serene as black coffee . . .

Whose unction can intercede for the dead?
Whose tongue is toothless enough to speak their piece?

What we are given in dreams we write as blue paint,
Or messages to the clouds.
At evening we wait for the rain to fall and the sky to clear.
Our words are words for the clay, uttered in undertones,
Our gestures salve for the wind.

We sit out on the earth and stretch our limbs,
Hoarding the little mounds of sorrow laid up in our hearts.

Self-Portrait

Someday they'll find me out, and my lavish hands,
Full moon at my back, fog groping the gone horizon, the edge
Of the continent scored in yellow, expectant lights,
White shoulders of surf, a wolf-colored sand,
The ashes and bits of char that will clear my name.

Till then, I'll hum to myself and settle the whereabouts.
Jade plants and oleander float in a shine.
The leaves of the pepper tree turn green.
My features are sketched with black ink in a slow drag through the sky,
Waiting to be filled in.

Hand that lifted me once, lift me again,
Sort me and flesh me out, fix my eyes.
From the mulch and the undergrowth, protect me and pass me on.
From my own words and my certainties,
From the rose and the easy cheek, deliver me, pass me on.

Mount Caribou at Night

Just north of the Yaak River, one man sits bolt upright,
A little bonnet of dirt and bunch grass above his head:
Northwestern Montana is hard relief,
And harder still the lying down and the rising up . . .

I speak to the others there, lodged in their stone wedges, the blocks
And slashes that vein the ground, and tell them that Walter Smoot,
Starched and at ease in his bony duds
Under the tamaracks, still holds the nightfall between his knees.

Work stars, drop by inveterate drop, begin
Cassiopeia's sails and electric paste
Across the sky. And down
Toward the cadmium waters that carry them back to the dawn,

They squeeze out Andromeda and the Whale,
Everything on the move, everything flowing and folding back
And starting again,
Star-slick, the flaking and crusting duff at my feet,

Smoot and Runyan and August Binder
Still in the black pulse of the earth, cloud-gouache
Over the tree line, Mount Caribou
Massive and on the rise and taking it in. And taking it back

To the future we occupied, and will wake to again, ourselves
And our children's children snug in our monk's robes,
Pushing the cauly hoods back, ready to walk out
Into the same night and the meadow grass, in step and on time.

Self-Portrait

Charles on the Trevisan, night bridge
To the crystal, infinite alphabet of his past.
Charles on the San Trovaso, earmarked,
Holding the pages of a thrown-away book, dinghy the color of honey
Under the pine boughs, the water east-flowing.

The wind will edit him soon enough,
And squander his broken chords
                        in tiny striations above the air,
No slatch in the undertow.
The sunlight will bear him out,
Giving him breathing room, and a place to lie.

And why not? The reindeer still file through the bronchial trees,
Holding their heads high.
The mosses still turn, the broomstraws flash on and off.
Inside, in the crosslight, and St. Jerome
And his creatures . . . St. Augustine, striking the words out.

Holy Thursday

Begins with the *ooo ooo* of a mourning dove
In the pepper tree, crack
Of blue and a flayed light on the hills,
Myself past the pumpkin blooms and out in the disced field,
Blake's children still hunched in sleep, dollops
Of bad dreams and an afterlife.
Canticles rise in spate from the bleeding heart.
Cathedrals assemble and disappear in the water beads.
I scuff at the slick adobe, one eye
On the stalk and one on the aftermath.

There's always a time for rust,
For looking down at the earth and its lateral chains.
There's always a time for the grass, teeming
Its little four-cornered purple flowers,
                                    tricked out in an oozy shine.
There's always a time for the dirt.
Reprieve, reprieve, the flies drone, their wings
Increasingly incandescent above the corn silk.
No answer from anything, four crows
On a eucalyptus limb, speaking in tongues.
No answer for them, either.

It's noon in the medlar tree, the sun
Sifting its glitter across the powdery stems.
It doesn't believe in God
And still is absolved.
It doesn't believe in God
And seems to get by, going from here to there.

Butterflies blow like pieces of half-burned construction paper over the
   sweet weeds,
And take what is given them.
Some hummer is luckier
Downwind, and smells blood, and seeks me out.

The afternoon hangs by a leaf.
The vines are a green complaint
From the slaking adobe dust. I settle and stand back.
The hawk realigns herself.
Splatter of mockingbird notes, a brief trill from the jay.
The fog starts in, breaking its various tufts loose.
Everything smudges and glows,
Cactus, the mustard plants and the corn,
Through the white reaches of four o'clock . . .
There's always a time for words.

Surf sounds in the palm tree,
Susurrations, the wind
                      making a big move from the west,
The children asleep again, their second selves
Beginning to stir, the moon
Lopsided, sliding their ladder down.
From under the billowing dead, from their wet hands and a saving
   grace,
The children begin to move, an angle of phosphorescence
Along the ridgeline.
                      Angels
Are counting cadence, their skeletal songs
What the hymns say, the first page and the last.

Self-Portrait

The pictures in the air have few visitors.

Sun drops past tie-post in the east shallows,
Moon rises to camera range. Over the zodiac,
The numbers and definitions arc,
Hiwassee at low tide, my brother one step up the cleared slope.

Winter on top of the Matterhorn,
Sun-goggled, standing the way our father stood, hands half in his
    pockets.
Behind him, the summer Alps
Fall down and away, little hillocks of white on the noon sky
Hiding their crosses, keeping the story straight.

Like Munch, I languish, my left cheek in my left palm,
Omniscient above the bay,
Checking the evidence, the postcards and the photographs,
O'Grady's finger pointing me out . . .

Madonna of Tenderness, Lady of Feints and Xs, you point too.

16)

Virginia Reel

In Clarke County, the story goes, the family name
Was saved by a single crop of wheat,
The houses and land kept in a clear receipt for the subsequent suicides,
The hard times and non-believers to qualify and disperse:
Woodburn and Cedar Hall, Smithfield, Auburn and North Hill:
Names like white moths kicked up from the tall grass,
Spreading across the countryside
From the Shenandoah to Charles Town and the Blue Ridge.

And so it happened. But none of us lives here now, in any of them,
Though Aunt Roberta is still in town,
Close to the place my great-great-grandfather taught Nelly Custis's
    children once
Answers to Luther. And Cardinal Newman too.
Who cares? Well, I do. It's worth my sighs
To walk here, on the wrong road, tracking a picture back
To its bricks and its point of view.
It's worth my while to be here, crumbling this dirt through my bare
    hands.

I've come back for the first time in twenty years,
Sand in my shoes, my pockets full of the same wind
That brought me before, my flesh
Remiss in the promises it made then, the absolutes it's heir to.
This is the road they drove on. And this is the rise
Their blood repaired to, removing its gloves.
And this is the dirt their lives were made of, the dirt the world is,
Immeasurable emptiness of all things.

I stand on the porch of Wickliffe Church,
My kinfolk out back in the bee-stitched vines and weeds,
The night coming on, my flat shirt drawing the light in,
Bright bud on the branch of nothing's tree.
In the new shadows, memory starts to shake out its dark cloth.
Everyone settles down, transparent and animate,
Under the oak trees.
Hampton passes the wine around, Jaq toasts to our health.

And when, from the blear and glittering air,
A hand touches my shoulder,
I want to fall to my knees, and keep on falling, here,
Laid down by the articles that bear my names,
The limestone and marble and locust wood.
But that's for another life. Just down the road, at Smithfield, the last of
    the apple blossoms
Fishtails to earth through the shot twilight,
A little vowel for the future, a signal from us to them.

Self-Portrait

Marostica, Val di Ser. Bassano del Grappa.
Madonna del Ortolo. San Giorgio, arc and stone.
The foothills above the Piave.

Places and things that caught my eye, Walt,
In Italy. On foot, Great Cataloguer, some twenty-odd years ago.

San Zeno and Caffè Dante. Catullus' seat.
Lake Garda. The Adige at Ponte Pietra
—I still walk there, a shimmer across the bridge on hot days,
The dust, for a little while, lying lightly along my sleeve—
Piazza Erbe, the twelve Apostles . . .

Over the grave of John Keats
The winter night comes down, her black habit starless and edged with
        ice,
Pure breaths of those who are rising from the dead.

Dino Campana, Arthur Rimbaud.
Hart Crane and Emily Dickinson. The Black Château.

Called Back

Friday arrives with all its attendant ecstasies.
Mirrors bloom in the hushed beds.

The ocotillo starts to extend
                    its orange tongues
Down in Sonora, the cactus puts on its beads.
Juan Quesada's Angel of Death, socket and marrow bone,
Stares from its cage and scorched eyes.

I've made my overtures to the Black Dog, and backed off.
I've touched the links in its gold chain.
I've called out and bent down and even acknowledged my own face.

Darkness, O Father of Charity, lay on your hands.

For over an hour the joy of the mockingbird has altered the leaves.
Stealthily, blossoms have settled along the bougainvillaea like purple
        moths
Catching their breaths, the sky still warm to the touch.
Nothing descends like snow or stiff wings
Out of the night.
                    Only the dew falls, soft as the footsteps of the dead.

Language can do just so much,
                    a flurry of prayers,
A chatter of glass beside the road's edge,
Flash and a half-glint as the headlights pass . . .

When the oak tree and the Easter grass have taken my body,
I'll start to count out my days, beginning at one.

Self-Portrait

In Murray, Kentucky, I lay once
On my side, the ghost-weight of a past life in my arms,
A life not mine. I know she was there,
Asking for nothing, heavy as bad luck, still waiting to rise.
I know now and I lift her.

Evening becomes us.
I see myself in a tight dissolve, and answer to no one.
Self-traitor, I smuggle in
The spider love, undoer and rearranger of all things.
Angel of Mercy, strip me down.

This world is a little place,
Just red in the sky before the sun rises.
Hold hands, hold hands
That when the birds start, none of us is missing.
Hold hands, hold hands.

Composition in Grey and Pink

The souls of the day's dead fly up like birds, big sister,
The sky shutters and casts loose.
And faster than stars the body goes to the earth.

Heat hangs like a mist from the trees.
Butterflies pump through the banked fires of late afternoon.
The rose continues its sure rise to the self.

Ashes, trampled garlands . . .

I dream of an incandescent space
                              where nothing distinct exists,
And where nothing ends, the days sliding like warm milk through the
    clouds,
Everyone's name in chalk letters once and for all,

The dogstar descending with its pestilent breath . . .

Fatherless, stiller than still water,
I want to complete my flesh
                        and sit in a quiet corner
Untied from God, where the dead don't sing in their sleep.

Laguna Blues

It's Saturday afternoon at the edge of the world.
White pages lift in the wind and fall.
Dust threads, cut loose from the heart, float up and fall.
Something's off-key in my mind.
Whatever it is, it bothers me all the time.

It's hot, and the wind blows on what I have had to say.
I'm dancing a little dance.
The crows pick up a thermal that angles away from the sea.
I'm singing a little song.
Whatever it is, it bothers me all the time.

It's Saturday afternoon and the crows glide down,
Black pages that lift and fall.
The castor beans and the pepper plant trundle their weary heads.
Something's off-key and unkind.
Whatever it is, it bothers me all the time.

October

The leaves fall from my fingers.
Cornflowers scatter across the field like stars,
                                        like smoke stars,
By the train tracks, the leaves in a drift

Under the slow clouds
                    and the nine steps to heaven,
The light falling in great sheets through the trees,
Sheets almost tangible.

The transfiguration will start like this, I think,
                                        breathless,
Quick blade through the trees,
Something with red colors falling away from my hands,

The air beginning to go cold . . .
                            And when it does
I'll rise from this tired body, a blood-knot of light,
Ready to take the darkness in.

—Or for the wind to come
And carry me, bone by bone, through the sky,
Its wafer a burn on my tongue,
                            its wine deep forgetfulness.

Childhood's Body

This is a rope of stars tied to my wrist.
This is a train, pulling the feckless palmprints of the dead.

It isn't enough to sing and begin again.
It isn't enough to dissemble the alphabet

And listen for
The one heartbeat I listen for,
                        as it comes as it goes,
Keeping the world alive,

My poems in a language now
                        I finally understand,
Little tablets of salt rubbed smooth by the wind.

It isn't enough to transform the curlicues.

(Deep water is what the albums will manifest,
                        the light jagged then not jagged,
The moon dragging her hooks
Through the lakes and the riverbeds . . .)

This is a lip of snow and a lip of blood.

Driving through Tennessee

It's strange what the past brings back.
Our parents, for instance, how ardently they still loom
In the brief and flushed
Fleshtones of memory, one foot in front of the next
Even in retrospect, and so unimpeachable.

And towns that we lived in once,
And who we were then, the roads we went back and forth on
Returning ahead of us like rime
In the moonlight's fall, and Jesus returning, and Stephen Martyr
And St. Paul of the Sword . . .

—I am their music,
Mothers and fathers and places we hurried through in the night:
I put my mouth to the dust and sing their song.
Remember us, Galeoto, and whistle our tune, when the time comes,
For charity's sake.

Spring Abstract

The notes I fall for fall from the lip of the sky,
A thousand years of music unstrung by the wind.
What do I care for the noun and its adjective?
What do I care for the quick shimmer that comes
Like a burning line so quietly toward me across the lake?

The green gloves of the fig tree unfold in the sun.
Jonquils slit from their shells.
And the bees plunder, glistening in and out
As they drag the Queens of the Night and the lime blossoms,
Rubbing the sleep from their eyes . . .

The hair of the full moon is pulled back.
The shrink of the warmed dew breaks off on the blades,
One line in the page that heaven and earth make.
Meager and rumpled, wrung out,
The poem is ground down from a mumbled joy.

Landscape with Seated Figure and Olive Trees

Orange blossoms have dropped their threads
On the stone floor of the heart
                              more often than once
Between last night's stars and last night's stars.
And the Preludes have left their rings
On the chalk white of the walls.
                         And the slide-harp has played and played.

And now, under the fruit trees,
                         the olives silver then not silver, the wind
In them then not, the old man
Sits in the sunfall,
Slouched and at ease in the sunfall, the leaves tipped in the wind.

The world is nothing to him.
And the music is nothing to him, and the noon sun.
Only the wind matters.
Only the wind as it moves through the tin shine of the leaves.
And the orange blossoms,
                    scattered like poems on the smooth stones.

Dog Yoga

A spring day in the weeds.
A thread of spittle across the sky, and a thread of ash.
Mournful cadences from the clouds.

Through the drives and the cypress beds,
$\qquad\qquad\qquad\qquad$ twenty-five years of sad news.

Mother of Thrushes, Our Lady of Crows,
Brief as a handkerchief,
$\qquad\qquad\qquad$ twenty-five years of sad news.

Later, stars and sea winds in and out of the open window.

Later, and lonesome among the sleepers,
$\qquad\qquad\qquad\qquad$ the day's thunder in hidden places,
One lissome cheek a notch in the noontide's leash,

A ghostly rain of sunlight among the ferns.

Year in, year out, the same loom from the dark.
Year in, year out, the same sound in the wind.

Near dawn, the void in the heart,
The last coat of lacquer along the leaves,
$\qquad\qquad\qquad\qquad$ the quench in the west.

California Spring

At dawn the dove croons.
A hawk hangs over the field.
The liquidambar rinses its hundred hands.

And the light comes on in the pepper trees.
Under its flat surfaces horns and noises are starting up.
The dewdrops begin to shrink.

How sad the morning is.
There is a tree which rains down in the field.
There is a spider that swings back and forth on his thin strings in the
     heart.

How cold the wind is.
And the sun is, caught like a kite in the drooped limbs of the tree.
The apricot blossoms scatter across the ice plant.

One angel dangles his wing.
The grass edges creak and the tide pools begin to shine.
Nothing forgives.

Laguna Dantesca

I want, like a little boat, to be isolate,
                              slipping across one element
Toward the horizon, whose lips know something but stay sealed
                              under the heaven of the moon.

There's something I want to look on, face to face.

Like a rock, or some other heavy thing, I want to descend through
        clear water
Endlessly,
        disappearing as she did,
Line after leached line, into the lunar deeps.

I want, like these lavender bells from the jacaranda tree,
To flare with the fixed stars,
                              used up and self-satisfied.

Tree frogs drum in the dark. The small brass of the natural world
Is drumming and what I want
                              is nothing to them.

Above me, the big dog lies low in the southern sky and bides its time.

Like a scrap of charred paper, I want to return.
There's something I want to look on whose face
                              rises and falls like a flame.

I want to sit down there, the dog asleep at my feet.

Dog Day Vespers

Sun like an orange mousse through the trees,
A snowfall of trumpet bells on the oleander;
                                        mantis paws
Craning out of the new wisteria; fruit smears in the west . . .
DeStael knifes a sail on the bay;
A mother's summons hangs like a towel on the dusk's hook.

Everything drips and spins
In the pepper trees, the pastel glide of the evening
Slowing to mother-of-pearl and the night sky.
Venus breaks clear in the third heaven.
Quickly the world is capped, and the seal turned.

I drag my chair to the deck's edge and the blue ferns.
I'm writing you now by flashlight,
The same news and the same story I've told you often before.
As the stag-stars begin to shine,
A wing brushes my left hand,
                              but it's not my wing.

Portrait of the Artist

with Hart Crane

It's Venice, late August, outside after lunch, and Hart
Is stubbing his cigarette butt in a wineglass,
The look on his face pre-moistened and antiseptic,
A little like death or a smooth cloud.
The watery light of his future still clings in the pergola.

The subject of all poems is the clock,
I think, those tiny, untouchable hands that fold across our chests
Each night and unfold each morning, finger by finger,
Under the new weight of the sun.
One day more is one day less.

I've been writing this poem for weeks now
With a pencil made of rain, smudging my face
And my friend's face, making a language where nothing stays.
The sunlight has no such desire.
In the small pools of our words, its business is radiance.

Portrait of the Artist

with Li Po

The "high heavenly priest of the White Lake" is now
A small mound in an endless plain of grass,
His pendants clicking and pearls shading his eyes.
He never said anything about the life after death,
Whose body is clothed in a blue rust and the smoke of dew.

He liked flowers and water most.
Everyone knows the true story of how he would write his verses and
    float them,
Like paper boats, downstream
                    just to watch them drift away.
Death never entered his poems, but rowed, with its hair down, far out
    on the lake,
Laughing and looking up at the sky.

Over a thousand years later, I write out one of his lines in a notebook,
The peach blossom follows the moving water,
And watch the October darkness gather against the hills.
All night long the river of heaven will move westward while no one
    notices.
The distance between the dead and the living
                    is more than a heartbeat and a breath.

The Monastery at Vršac

We've walked the grounds,
                              inspected the vaults and the old church,
Looked at the icons and carved stalls,

And followed the path to the bishop's grave.

Now we sit in the brandy-colored light of late afternoon
Under the locust trees,
                              attended and small
From the monastery. Two nuns hop back and forth like grackles
Along the path. The light drips from the leaves.

Little signals of dust rise uninterpreted from the road.
The grass drones in its puddle of solitude.

The stillness is awful, as though from the inside of a root . . .

—Time's sluice and the summer rains erode our hearts
                              and carry our lives away.
We hold what we can in our two hands,
Sinking, each year, another inch in the earth . . .

Mercy upon us,
                    we who have learned to preach but not to pray.

Dead Color

I lie for a long time on my left side and my right side
And eat nothing,
                        but no voice comes on the wind
And no voice drops from the cloud.
Between the grey spiders and the orange spiders,
                                no voice comes on the wind . . .

Later, I sit for a long time by the waters of Har,
And no face appears on the face of the deep.

Meanwhile, the heavens assemble their dark map.
The traffic begins to thin.
Aphids munch on the sweet meat of the lemon trees.
The lawn sprinklers rise and fall . . .

And here's a line of brown ants cleaning a possum's skull.
And here's another, come from the opposite side.

Over my head, star-pieces dip in their yellow scarves toward their black
    desire.

Windows, rapturous windows!

Hawaii Dantesca

White-sided flowers are thrusting up on the hillside,
                                        blank love letters from the dead.
It's autumn, and nobody seems to mind.

Or the broken shadows of those missing for hundreds of years
Moving over the sugar cane
                                        like storks, which nobody marks or mends.

This is the story line.

And the viridescent shirtwaists of light the trees wear.
And the sutra-circles of cattle egrets wheeling out past the rain showers.
And the spiked marimbas of dawn rattling their amulets . . .

Soon it will be time for the long walk under the earth toward the sea.

And time to retrieve the yellow sunsuit and little shoes
                                        they took my picture in
In Knoxville, in 1938.

Time to gather the fire in its quartz bowl.

I hope the one with the white wings will come.
I hope the island of reeds is as far away as I think it is.

When I get there, I hope they forgive me if the knot I tie is the wrong
    knot.

Ars Poetica

I like it back here

Under the green swatch of the pepper tree and the aloe vera.
I like it because the wind strips down the leaves without a word.
I like it because the wind repeats itself,

                           and the leaves do.

I like it because I'm better here than I am there,

Surrounded by fetishes and figures of speech:
Dog's tooth and whale's tooth, my father's shoe, the dead weight
Of winter, the inarticulation of joy . . .

The spirits are everywhere.

And once I have them called down from the sky, and spinning and
      dancing in the palm of my hand,
What will it satisfy?
                I'll still have

The voices rising out of the ground,
The fallen star my blood feeds,

                  this business I waste my heart on.

And nothing stops that.

Bar Giamaica, 1959–60

Grace is the focal point,
                 the tip ends of her loosed hair
Like match fire in the back light,
Her hands in a "Here's the church . . ."
                           She's looking at Ugo Mulas,
Who's looking at us.

Ingrid is writing this all down, and glances up, and stares hard.

This still isn't clear.

I'm looking at Grace, and Goldstein and Borsuk and Dick Venezia
Are looking at me.
                Yola keeps reading her book.

And that leaves the rest of them: Susan and Elena and Carl Glass.
And Thorp and Schimmel and Jim Gates,
                      and Hobart and Schneeman

One afternoon in Milan in the late spring.

Then Ugo finishes, drinks a coffee, and everyone goes away.
Summer arrives, and winter;
                     the snow falls and no one comes back
Ever again,
            all of them gone through the star filter of memory,
With its small gravel and metal tables and passers-by . . .

Gate City Breakdown

Like a vein of hard coal, it was the strike
We fantasized, the pocket of sure reward we sidestepped the roadblocks
    for
In southwest Virginia, seamed in its hillside
Above the North Fork of the Holston River.

One afternoon before Christmas
In 1953, we crossed the bridge from Tennessee on a whiskey run,
Churchill and Bevo Hammond and Philbeck and I,
All home for the holidays.
On the back road where they chased us, we left the Sheriff's Patrol in
    their own dust,
And washed ours down with Schlitz on the way home.

Jesus, it's so ridiculous, and full of self-love,
The way we remember ourselves,
                   and the dust we leave . . .

Remember me as you will, but remember me once
Slide-wheeling around the curves,
                letting it out on the other side of the line.

New Year's Eve, 1979

After the picture show, the explanation is usually found in
The moralistic overtones of our lives:
We are what we've always been,
Everybody uses somebody,
In the slow rise to the self, we're drawn up by many hands.

And so it is here.
                    Will Charles look on happiness in this life?
Will the past be the present ever again?
Will the dead abandon their burdens and walk to the riverbank?

In this place, at year's end, under a fitful moon, tide pools
Spindle the light.
Across their floors, like spiders,
Hermit crabs quarter and spin.
                    Their sky is a glaze and a day . . .

What matters to them is what comes up from below, and from out
    there
In the deep water,
            and where the deep water comes from.

Laguna Beach

41)

The Southern Cross

Things that divine us we never touch:

The black sounds of the night music,
The Southern Cross, like a kite at the end of its string,

And now this sunrise, and empty sleeve of a day,
The rain just starting to fall, and then not fall,

No trace of a story line.

———————

All day I've remembered a lake and a sudsy shoreline,
Gauze curtains blowing in and out of open windows all over the
      South.

It's 1936, in Tennessee. I'm one
And spraying the dead grass with a hose.
The curtains blow in and out.

And then it's not. And I'm not and they're not.

Or it's 1941 in a brown suit, or '53 in its white shoes,
Overlay after overlay tumbled and brought back,
As meaningless as the sea would be
                  if the sea could remember its waves . . .

———————

Nothing had told me my days were marked for a doom
                  under the cold stars of the Virgin.
Nothing had told me that woe would buzz at my side like a fly.

The morning is dark with spring.
The early blooms on the honeysuckle shine like maggots after the rain.
The purple mouths of the passion blossoms
                              open their white gums to the wind.

How sweet the past is, no matter how wrong, or how sad.
How sweet is yesterday's noise.

———————

All day the ocean was like regret,
                    clearing its throat, brooding and self-absorbed.

Now the wisteria tendrils extend themselves like swan's necks under
    Orion.

Now the small stars in the orange trees.

———————

At Garda, on Punto San Vigilio, the lake,
In springtime, is like the sea,
Wind fishtailing the olive leaves like slash minnows beneath the
    vineyards,
Ebb and flow of the sunset past Sirmio,
                         flat voice of the waters
Retelling their story, again and again, as though to unburden itself

Of an unforgotten guilt,
                  and not relieved
Under the soothing hand of the dark,

The clouds over Bardolino dragging the sky for the dead
Bodies of those who refuse to rise,
Their orange robes and flaming bodices trolling across the hills,

Nightwind by now in the olive trees,
No sound but the wind from anything
                         under the tired Italian stars . . .

43)

And the voice of the waters, starting its ghostly litany.

——————

River of sighs and forgetfulness
                    (and the secret light Campana saw),
River of bloom-bursts from the moon,
                    of slivers and broken blades from the moon
In an always-going-away of glints . . .

Dante and Can Grande once stood here,
Next to the cool breath of S. Anastasia,
                            watching the cypress candles
Flare in their deep green across the Adige
In the Giusti Gardens.
                  Before that, in his marble tier,
Catullus once sat through the afternoons.
Before that, God spoke in the rocks . . .

And now it's my turn to stand
Watching a different light do the same things on a different water,
The Adige bearing its gifts
                through the April twilight of 1961.

——————

When my father went soldiering, apes dropped from the trees.
When my mother wrote home from bed, the stars asked for a pardon.

They're both ghosts now, haunting the chairs and the sugar chest.

From time to time I hear their voices drifting like smoke through the
      living room,
Touching the various things they owned once.
Now they own nothing
               and drift like smoke through the living room.

——————

Thinking of Dante, I start to feel
What I think are wings beginning to push out from my shoulder
    blades,
And the firm pull of water under my feet.

Thinking of Dante, I think of La Pia,
                            and Charles Martel
And Cacciaguida inside the great flower of Paradise,
And the thin stem of Purgatory
                    rooted in Hell.

Thinking of Dante is thinking about the other side,
And the other side of the other side.
It's thinking about the noon noise and the daily light.

———————

Here is the truth. The wind rose, the sea
Shuffled its blue deck and dealt you a hand:
Blank, blank, blank, blank, blank.
Pelicans rode on the flat back of the waves through the green
    afternoon.
Gulls malingered along its breezes.
The huge cross of an airplane's shadow hurried across the sand,
                            but no one stayed on it
For long, and nobody said a word.
You could see the island out past the orange gauze of the smog.

———————

The Big Dipper has followed me all the days of my life.
Under its tin stars my past has come and gone.
Tonight, in the April glaze
                    and scrimshaw of the sky,
It blesses me once again
With its black water, and sends me on.

———————

After twelve years it's hard to recall
That defining sound the canal made at sundown, slap
Of tide swill on the church steps,
Little runnels of boat wash slipping back from the granite slabs
In front of Toio's, undulant ripples
Flattening out in small hisses, the oily rainbows regaining their loose
      shapes
Silently, mewling and quick yelps of the gulls
Wheeling from shadow into the pink and grey light over the Zattere,
Lapping and rocking of water endlessly,
At last like a low drone in the dark shell of the ear
As the night lifted like mist from the Ogni Santi
And San Sebastiano
                into the cold pearl of the sky . . .

All that year it lullabied just outside my window
As Venice rode through my sleep like a great spider,
Flawless and Byzantine,
              webbed like glass in its clear zinc.
In winter the rain fell
              and the locust fell.
In summer the sun rose
Like a whetstone over the steel prows of the gondolas,
Their silver beak-blades rising and falling,
                  the water whiter than stone.
In autumn the floods came, and oil as thick as leaves in the entry way.
In spring, at evening, under the still-warm umbrellas,
We watched the lights blaze and extend
              along the rio,
And watched the black boats approaching, almost without sound.
And still the waters sang lullaby.

I remember myself as a figure among the colonnades,
Leaning from left to right,
              one hand in my pocket,
The way the light fell,
            the other one holding me up.

I remember myself as a slick on the slick canals,
Going the way the tide went,
The city sunk to her knees in her own reflection.
I remember the way that Pound walked

                        across San Marco
At *passeggiata*, as though with no one,

                             his eyes on the long ago.
I remember the time that Tate came.

                      And Palazzo Guggenheim
When the floods rose

                  and the boat took us all the way
Through the front doors and down to the back half
Of *da Montin*, where everyone was, clapping their hands.

What's hard to remember is how the wind moved and the reeds clicked
Behind Torcello,

                little bundles of wind in the marsh grass
Chasing their own tails, and skidding across the water.
What's hard to remember is how the electric lights
Were played back, and rose and fell on the black canal
Like swamp flowers,

                  shrinking and stretching,
Yellow and pale and iron-blue from the oil.
It's hard to remember the way the snow looked

                       on San Gregorio,
And melting inside the pitch tubs and the smoke of San Trovaso,
The gondolas beached and stripped,
The huge snowflakes planing down through the sea-heavy air
Like dead moths,

                drifting and turning . . .

———————

As always, silence will have the last word,
And Venice will lie like silk

                at the edge of the sea and the night sky,
Albescent under the moon.

Everyone's life is the same life
                              if you live long enough.

————————

Orioles shuttle like gold thread
                              through the grey cloth of daylight.
The fog is so low and weighted down
Crows fall through like black notes from the sky.
The orioles stitch and weave.
Somewhere below, the ocean nervously grinds its teeth
As the morning begins to take hold
                              and the palm trees gleam.

————————

There is an otherness inside us
We never touch,
                    no matter how far down our hands reach.
It is the past,
                    with its good looks and *Anytime, Anywhere* . . .
Our prayers go out to it, our arms go out to it
Year after year,
But who can ever remember enough?

————————

Friday again, with its sack of bad dreams
And long-legged birds,
                         a handful of ashes for this and that
In the streets, and some for the squat piano.

Friday beneath the sky, its little postcards of melancholy
Outside each window,
                         the engines inside the roses at half speed,
The huge page of the sea with its one word *despair*,

Fuchsia blossoms littered across the deck,
Unblotted tide pools of darkness beneath the ferns . . .
And still I go on looking,
                         match after match in the black air.

———————

The lime, electric green of the April sea
                         off Ischia
Is just a thumb-rub on the window glass between here and there:
And the cloud cap above the volcano
That didn't move when the sea wind moved;
And the morning the doves came, low from the mountain's shadow,
                                        under the sunlight,
Over the damp tops of the vine rows,
Eye-high in a scythe slip that dipped and rose and cut down toward the
        sea;
And the houses like candy wrappers blown up against the hillside
Above Sant'Angelo,
                         fuchsia and mauve and cyclamen;
And the story Nicola told,
How the turtle doves come up from Africa
On the desert winds,
                         how the hunters take the fresh seeds
From their crops and plant them,
The town windows all summer streaked with the nameless blooms.

The landscape was always the best part.

———————

Places swim up and sink back, and days do,
The edges around what really happened
                                        we'll never remember
No matter how hard we stare back at the past:

One April, in downtown Seville,
                         alone on an Easter morning
Wasted in emerald light from the lemon trees,

49)

I watched a small frog go back and forth on the lily pads
For hours, and still don't know
                    just what I was staying away from . . .

(And who could forget Milano in '59,
                            all winter under the rain?
Cathedrals for sure,
And dry stops in the Brera,
                    all of her boulevards ending in vacant lots.

And Hydra and Mykonos,
Barely breaking the calm with their white backs
As they roll over
                    and flash back down to the dark . . .)

Places swim up and sink back, and days do,
Larger and less distinct each year,
As we are,
                    and lolling about in the same redress,
Leaves and insects drifting by on their windows.

Rome was never like that,
                    and the Tiber was never like that,
Nosing down from the Apennines,
                    color of *café-au-lait* as it went through town . . .

Still, I can't remember the name of one street
                            near Regina Coeli,
Or one block of the Lungotevere on either side,
Or one name of one shop on Campo dei Fiori.
Only Giordano Bruno,
                    with his razed look and black caul,
Rises unbidden out of the blank
Unruffled waters of memory,
                            his martyred bronze
Gleaming and still wet in the single electric light.

I can't remember the colors I said I'd never forget
On Via Giulia at sundown,
The ochers and glazes and bright hennas of each house,
Or a single day from November of 1964.
I can't remember the way the stairs smelled
                                        or the hallway smelled
At Piazza del Biscione.
                        Or just how the light fell
Through the east-facing window over the wicker chairs there.

I do remember the way the boar hung
                                in the butcher shop at Christmas
Two streets from the Trevi fountain, a crown of holly and mistletoe
Jauntily over his left ear.
I do remember the flower paintings
Nodding throughout the May afternoons
                                on the dining-room walls
At Zajac's place.
                And the reliquary mornings,
And Easter, and both Days of the Dead . . .

At noon in the English Cemetery no one's around.
Keats is off to the left, in an open view.
Shelley and Someone's son are straight up ahead.

With their marble breath and their marble names,
                                the sun in a quick squint through the trees,
They lie at the edge of everywhere,
                        Rome like a stone cloud at the back of their eyes.

————————

Time is the villain in most tales,
                        and here, too,
Lowering its stiff body into the water.
Its landscape is the resurrection of the word,
No end of it,
                the petals of wreckage in everything.

I've been sitting here tracking the floor plan
                                        of a tiny, mottled log spider
Across the front porch of the cabin,
And now she's under my chair,
                            off to her own devices,
Leaving me mine, and I start watching the two creeks

Come down through the great meadow
Under the lodgepole pine and the willow run,
The end of June beginning to come clear in the clouds,
Shadows like drowned men where the creeks go under the hill.

Last night, in the flood run of the moon, the bullbats
Diving out of the yellow sky
                            with their lonesome and jungly whistling,
I watched, as I've watched before, the waters send up their smoke
        signals of blue mist,
And thought, for the first time,
                        I half-understood what they keep on trying to say.

But now I'm not sure.
                        Behind my back, the spider has got her instructions
And carries them out.
Flies drone, wind back-combs the marsh grass, swallows bank and
        climb.
Everything I can see knows just what to do,

Even the dragonfly, hanging like lapis lazuli in the sun . . .

                    _____

I can't remember enough.

How the hills, for instance, at dawn in Kingsport
In late December in 1962 were black
                            against a sky

The color of pale fish blood and water that ran to white
As I got ready to leave home for the hundredth time,
My mother and father asleep,
                              my sister asleep,
Carter's Valley as dark as the inside of a bone
Below the ridge,
                the first knobs of the Great Smokies
Beginning to stick through the sunrise,
The hard pull of a semi making the grade up U.S. 11W,
The cold with its metal teeth ticking against the window,
The long sigh of the screen door stop,
My headlights starting to disappear
                              in the day's new turning . . .

I'll never be able to.

                    ————————

Sunday, a brute bumblebee working the clover tops
Next to the step I'm sitting on,
                          sticking his huge head
Into each tiny, white envelope.
The hot sun of July, in the high Montana air, bastes a sweet glaze
On the tamarack and meadow grass.
In the blue shadows
                  moist curls of the lupine glide
And the bog lilies extinguish their mellow lamps . . .

Sunday, a *Let us pray* from the wind, a glint
Of silver among the willows.
                        The lilacs begin to bleed
In their new sleep, and the golden vestments of morning
Lift for a moment, then settle back into place.
The last of the dog roses offers itself by the woodpile.
Everything has its work,
                      everything written down
In a secondhand grace of solitude and tall trees . . .

———————

August licks at the pine trees.
Sun haze, and little fugues from the creek.
Fern-sleep beneath the green skirt of the marsh.

I always imagine a mouth
Starting to open its blue lips
Inside me, an arm
                          curving sorrowfully over an open window
At evening, and toads leaping out of the wet grass.

Again the silence of flowers.
Again the faint notes of piano music back in the woods.
How easily summer fills the room.

———————

The life of this world is wind.
Windblown we come, and windblown we go away.
All that we look on is windfall.
All we remember is wind.

———————

Pickwick was never the wind . . .

It's what we forget that defines us, and stays in the same place,
And waits to be rediscovered.
Somewhere in all that network of rivers and roads and silt hills,
A city I'll never remember,
                          its walls the color of pure light,
Lies in the August heat of 1935,
In Tennessee, the bottomland slowly becoming a lake.
It lies in a landscape that keeps my imprint

Forever,
          and stays unchanged, and waits to be filled back in.
Someday I'll find it out
And enter my old outline as though for the first time,

And lie down, and tell no one.

THE OTHER SIDE OF THE RIVER

(1984)

Lost Bodies

Last night I thought of Torri del Benaco again,
Its almond trees in blossom,
                            its cypresses clothed in their dark fire,

And the words carved on that concrete cross

I passed each day of my life
In Kingsport going to town
            GET RIGHT WITH GOD / JESUS IS COMING SOON.

If I had it all to do over again
                            I'd be a Medievalist.
I'd thoroughly purge my own floor.

Something's for sure in the clouds, but it's not for me,

Though all the while that light tips the fast-moving water,
East wind in a rush through the almond trees.

_____

The cross was opposite Fleenor's Cabins below the hill
On U.S. 11W.
Harold Shipley told me, when I was twelve,
                            he'd seen a woman undressed

In the back seat of a Buick, between two men,
                            her cunt shaved clean,
In front of the motel office.
They gave him a dollar, he said, to stick his finger up there.

59)

What can you say to that?
                    everything Jesus promised

(My five senses waiting apart in their grey hoods,
Touching their beads,
                    licking the ashes that stained their lips)

And someone to tell it to.

                    ———————

Torri del Benaco, on the east side of Lake Garda,
Was north past Peschiera and San Vigilio,
                    under the Bardolino hills.
I seldom went there, and remember it poorly.

One Sunday, I drove through town on my way to Riva at the top of
    the lake.
An east wind was blowing out toward the water,

Down through the vineyards, and down through the trees at the lake's
    edge.

I remember the cypress nods in its warm breath.
I remember the almond blossoms
                    floating out on the waves, west to Salò.
I remember the way they looked there,
                    a small flotilla of matches.

I remember their flash in the sun's flare.

                    ———————

You've got to sign your name to something, it seems to me.
And so we rephrase the questions
Endlessly,
        hoping the answer might somehow change.

Still, a piece of his heart is not a piece of your heart,
Sweet Jesus, and never will be, but stays
A little window into the past,
                                increasingly licked transparent
And out of shape.

When you die, you fall down,
                                you don't rise up
Like a scrap of burnt paper into the everlasting.
Each morning we learn this painfully,
                pulling our bodies up by the roots from their deep sleep.

———————

Nobody takes that road now.
                                The tourist cabins are gone,
And Harold, and Rose Dials
Who lived in a tarpaper shack just off the highway,
Nailed hard to the mountainside.
                                And the two men and the Buick too,
Long gone down the Interstate
And the satellites that have taken us all from town.

Only the cross is still there, sunk deeper into the red clay
Than anyone could have set it.

And that luminous, nameless body whose flesh takes on
The mottoes we say we live by . . .

———————

Of all the places around the lake,
                                I've loved Sirmione best,
Its brilliant winks in the sun
And glassy exceptions like a trace in the mind.

Others stay in the memory like pieces of songs
You think you remember but don't,
                                    only a phrase here and there
Surfacing as it should, and in tune.

Gardone and Desenzano are like that, and Torri del Benaco.

Mostly what I remember is one garden, outside the town of Garda,
Between the lake's edge and the road:
Corn and beans, it looked like, and squash and finocchio.

———————

All things that come to him come under his feet
In a glorious body,
                        they say. And why not?
It beats the alternative, the mighty working
Set to subdue the celestial flesh.

And does so, letting the grass go stiff, and the needles brown,

Letting the dirt take over. This is as far as it goes,
Where deer browse the understory and jays
                                            leap through the trees,

Where chainsaws
Whittle away at the darkness, and diesel rigs
Carry our deaths all night through the endless rain.

Lost Souls

From the bad eye and early morning
                                    you raise me
Unshuttered from the body of ashes
                                    you raise me
Out of the dust and moth light
                                    memory
Into the undertow of my own life
                                    you make me remember

———————

I never dreamed of anything as a child.
I just assumed it was all next door,
                                    or day-after-tomorrow at least,
A different shirt I'd put on when the time was right.

It hasn't worked out that way.

My father wrote out his dreams on lined paper, as I do now,
And gave them up to the priest
                                    for both to come to terms with.
I give you mine for the same reason,

To summon the spirits up and set the body to music.

———————

The last time I saw George Vaughan,
He was standing in front of my father's casket at the laying out,
One of the kindest men I've ever known.

When I was sixteen, he taught me the way to use a jackhammer,
                                        putting the hand grip
Into my stomach and clinching down,
Riding it out till the jarring became a straight line.

He taught me the way a shovel breathes,
And how the red clay gives away nothing.
He took my hand when my hand needed taking.

And I didn't even remember his name.

———————

One evening in 1957 I found myself outside of Nashville,
                                        face down on the ground,
A straw in my mouth, the straw stuck deep
In the ginned heart of a watermelon,
                                the faces of five friends
Almost touching my face
As we sucked the sweet gin as fast as we could.

Over the green hinge of the Cumberland Plateau
The eyelash dusk of July was coming down
                                effortlessly, smooth as an oiled joint.
Agnes rolled over and looked up at the sky.
Her cousin, our host, rolled over and looked up at the sky.

What a life, he said. Jesus, he said, what a life.

———————

Nobody needs to remember the Kingsport *Times-News*
In the summer of 1953,
                but I do,
Disguised to myself as a newspaperman on my slow way
To the city jail to check the drunk tank,
                                full summer and after supper,
Korea just over, the neon of Wallace's News and Parks-Belk
Lying along the sidewalk like tear sheets of tinted plastic,

Across Center and down to Freel's Drug,
                                    then left, and then left again
Into the blowing shadow and light
Under the elm trees,
The world and its disregard in the palm of my hand.

Nobody needs to remember the smell of bay rum
And disinfectant,
                    the desperate grey faces
Of dirt farmers caught in the wrong dark at the wrong time,
Bib overalls sour with sweat and high water,
Brogans cracked and half broken,
                                    the residue
Of all our illuminations and unnamed lives . . .
At least I thought that then.
And nobody needs to remember any of that,
                                    but I do.

What *does* one do with one's life? A shelf-and-a-half
Of magazines, pictures on all the walls
Of the way I was, and everyone standing next to me?
This one, for instance for instance for instance . . .

Nothing's like anything else in the long run.
Nothing you write down is ever as true as you think it was.

But so what? Churchill and I and Bill Ring
Will still be chasing that same dead pintail duck
                                    down the same rapids in 1951
Of the Holston River. And Ted Glynn
Will be running too.
                    And 1951 will always be 1951.

A little curtain of flesh, Blake said,
For his own reasons . . .

65)

And I had mine to draw it last night on the Wasatch Range
And pull it back as the sun rose
                            over the north fork
And blue weave of the Cumberlands.
It was June again, and 1964 again,
                            and I still wasn't there
As they laid her down and my father turned away,
I still imagine, precisely, into the cave of cold air
He lived in for eight more years, the cars
Below my window in Rome honking maniacally
                            O still small voice of calm . . .

Lonesome Pine Special

I was walking out this morning with rambling on my mind.
—SARA CARTER

There's a curve in the road, and a slow curve in the land,
Outside of Barbourville, Kentucky, on U.S. 25E,
I've always liked
                    each time I've passed it,
Bottomland, river against a ridge to the west,
A few farmhouses on each side of the road, some mailboxes
Next to a dirt lane that leads off through the fields.
Each time I'd think
                    How pleasant it must be to live here.

————————

In Kingsport, when I was growing up,
Everyone seemed to go to Big Stone Gap, Virginia, up U.S. 23,
All the time.
                    Everyone had an uncle or aunt there,
Or played golf, or traded cars.
They were always going up there
                              to get married, or get liquor,
Or to get what was owed them
By someone they'd been in the service with.

Lone went up there more often than anyone else did,
Part of his territory for State Farm,
                              somebody said,
Without much conviction.

When the talk turned to whiskey,
                    and everyone dusted his best lie off,
We all knew, or thought we knew, where Lone went
With his funny walk and broken back

He could hit a golf ball a ton with,
                              even if he did stand sideways
Like a man hauling a body out of the water,
Being the real owner, we thought, of that gas station out on the
      Jonesboro highway
You went to the back of
                  for a pint after 10 p.m.,
Lone getting richer and richer until the Moose Lodge
Started to take his business away
                  by doing it legal, and during the daylight.

So Lone went back, we all thought,
To stumping around the golf course, still
Hitting it sideways, still selling whatever he could
To anyone foolish enough to play him and pay him,
Old Lone, slicker than owl oil.

———————

It was all so American,
The picket fence of wrought iron a hundred years old,
Lilacs at every corner of the lawned yard
                              in great heaps and folds,
A white house and wild alfalfa in scattered knots
Between the fence and the cracked sidewalk,
The wind from the Sawtooth Mountains
                  riffling the dust in slow eddies along the street
Near the end of June in Hailey, Idaho,
The house where Pound was born,
                              with its red maple floors
And small windows two blocks from Idaho 75,
Hemingway ten miles on up the same road between two evergreens,
Nobody noticing either place
                  as the cars went through town
All night and all day, going north, going south . . .

———————

Another landscape I liked
Was south of Wytheville, Virginia, on U.S. 52
Just short of the Carolina line,
                              a steel bridge over the New River,
Pasture on both sides of the road and woods on the easy slopes,
Big shrubs and trees lining the riverbanks like fur,
The road and the river both
Angling back toward the Iron Mountains,
The valley bulging out to the east
                              in a graceful swirl,
The dead chestnut trees like grey candles
Wherever the woods began . . .

What is it about a known landscape
                              that tends to undo us,
That shuffles and picks us out
For terminal demarcation, the way a field of lupine
Seen in profusion deep in the timber
Suddenly seems to rise like a lavender ground fog
At noon?
          What is it inside the imagination that keeps surprising us
At odd moments
                    when something is given back
We didn't know we had had
In solitude, spontaneously, and with great joy?

———————

Today, at midsummer noon, I took the wooden floats
To the Yaak River, the small ones I'd carved from the larch
And cedar chips,
                    and loosed them downstream
To carry my sins away, as the palace guardians did each year at this
    time
In medieval Japan,
Where the river goes under the new bridge
                              on County 508

And the first homesteaders took up their quarter sections.
From Sam Runyan's to Susie Speed's,
Through white water and rock and the tendrilous shade
Of the tamaracks,
                    out into rubbery blotches of sunlight,
The floats' shadows hanging beneath them like odd anchors
Along the pebbled bottom, the river slowing and widening,
The floats at great distances from one another
Past Binder's cabin under the black
                              of the evergreen-covered dam
And over the falls and gone into foam and next year . . .

————

In the world of dirt, each tactile thing
                              repeats the untouchable
In its own way, and in its own time.
Just short of Tryon, North Carolina, on U.S. 176,
Going south down the old Saluda Grade,
                              kudzu has grown up
And over the tops of miles of oak trees and pine trees,
A wall of vines a hundred feet high, or used to be,
Into South Carolina,
That would have gone for a hundred more with the right scaffolding,
Rising out of the rock and hard clay in thin, prickly ropes
To snake and thread in daily measurable distances
Over anything still enough long enough,
                              and working its way
Out of the darkness and overhang of its own coils
To break again and again
Into the sunlight, worthless and everywhere,
                              breathing, breathing,
Looking for leverage and a place to climb.

————

It's true, I think, as Kenkō says in his *Idleness*,
That all beauty depends upon disappearance,

The bitten edges of things,
                    the gradual sliding away
Into tissue and memory,
                    the uncertainty
And dazzling impermanence of days we beg our meanings from,
And their frayed loveliness.

Going west out of Kalispell, Montana, on U.S. 2,
If you turned off at Kila,
                    and skirted the big slough
Where Doagie Duncan killed three men some seventy years ago
After a fight over muskrat hides,
Then turned south toward the timber
                    and higher ground
On the dirt road to the Flathead Mine,
Past Sundelius' homestead and up toward Brown's Meadows,
Then swung down where the mine road
                    branches right and doubles back,
You'd come through the thinning spruce and fir
And lodgepole pine to the suddenly open hillsides
And deep draws
          of the Hog Heaven country
And start to see what I mean, the bunchgrass and bitterroot
And wild clover flattening under the wind
As you turned from the dirt road,
                    opened the Kansas gate
And began to follow with great care
The overgrown wagon ruts through the blowing field,
                    the huge tamarack snag,
Where the tracks end and the cabin is,
Black in the sunlight's wash and flow
                    just under the hill's crown,
Pulling you down like weight to the front door . . .

The cabin is still sizable, four rooms and the walls made
Of planed lumber inside,
                    the outside chinked with mud

71)

And cement, everything fifty years
Past habitation, the whole structure

                      leaning into the hillside,
Windowless, doorless, and oddly beautiful in its desolation
And attitude, and not like
The cold and isolate misery it must have stood for
When someone lived here, and heard, at night,
This same wind sluicing the jack pines

                      and ruined apple trees
In the orchard, and felt the immensity
Loneliness brings moving under his skin
Like a live thing, and emptiness everywhere like a live thing
Beyond the window's reach and fire's glare . . .

Whoever remembers that best owns all this now.
And after him it belongs to the wind again,

              and the shivering bunchgrass, and the seed cones.

———————

There is so little to say, and so much time to say it in.

Once, in 1955 on an icy road in Sam's Gap, North Carolina,
Going north into Tennessee on U.S. 23,
I spun out on a slick patch
And the car turned once-and-a-half around,
Stopping at last with one front wheel on a rock

                  and the other on air,
Hundreds of feet of air down the mountainside
I backed away from, mortal again
After having left myself

              and returned, having watched myself
Wrench the wheel toward the spin, as I'm doing now,
Stop and shift to reverse, as I'm doing now,

                and back out on the road
As I entered my arms and fingers again
Calmly, as though I had never left them,

Shift to low, and never question the grace
That had put me there and alive, as I'm doing now . . .

———————

Solo Joe is a good road.
It cuts southwest off Montana 508 above Blacktail Creek,
Crosses the East Fork of the Yaak River
                                    and climbs toward Mount Henry.
Joe was an early prospector
Back in the days when everything came in by pack string
Or didn't come in at all.
                          One spring he shot his pet cat
On the front porch with a rifle between the eyes
As she came through the cabin door.
He later explained she was coming for him
                                    but he got her first.
He drank deer's blood, it was said, and kept to himself,
Though one story has him a gambler later downriver near Kalispell.
Nobody lives there now,
But people still placer-mine in the summer, and camp out
Illegally on the riverbank.
No one knows anything sure about Joe but his first name
And the brown government sign that remembers him.
And that's not so bad, I think.
                          It's a good road, as I say,
And worse things than that will happen to most of us.

———————

The road in is always longer than the road out,
Even if it's the same road.
I think I'd like to find one
                          impassable by machine,
A logging road from the early part of the century,
Overgrown and barely detectable.
I'd like it to be in North Carolina,
                          in Henderson County

Between Mount Pinnacle and Mount Anne,
An old spur off the main track
The wagons and trucks hauled out on.
Blackberry brambles, and wild raspberry and poison ivy
Everywhere; grown trees between the faint ruts;
Deadfall and windfall and velvety sassafras fans
On both sides . . .
              It dips downhill and I follow it.
It dips down and it disappears and I follow it.

Two Stories

Tonight, on the deck, the lights
Semaphore up at me through the atmosphere,
Town lights, familiar lights
                          pulsing and slacking off
The way they used to back on the ridge outside of Kingsport
Thirty-five years ago,
The moonlight sitting inside my head
Like knives,
                the cold like a drug I knew I'd settle down with.
I used to imagine them shore lights, as these are, then,
As something inside me listened with all its weight
For the sea-surge and the sea-change.

—————

There's a soft spot in everything
Our fingers touch,
                   the one place where everything breaks
When we press it just right.
The past is like that with its arduous edges and blind sides,
The whorls of our fingerprints
                       embedded along its walls
Like fossils the sea has left behind.

—————

This is a story I swear is true.

I used to sleepwalk. But only
On camping trips,
                  or whenever I slept outside.
One August, when I was eleven, on Mount LeConte in Tennessee,

Campfire over, and ghost story over,
Everyone still asleep, apparently I arose
From my sleeping bag,
                          opened the tent flap, and started out on the trail
That led to the drop-off, where the mountainside
Went straight down for almost a thousand feet.
Half-moon and cloud cover, so some light
As I went on up the path through the rhododendron,
The small pebbles and split roots
                          like nothing under my feet.
The cliffside was half a mile from the campsite.
As I got closer,
              moving blindly, unerringly,
Deeper in sleep than the shrubs,
I stepped out, it appears,
Onto the smooth lip of the rock cape of the cliff,
When my left hand, and then my right hand,
Stopped me as they were stopped
By the breathing side of a bear which woke me
And there we were,
                the child and the black bear and the cliff-drop,
And this is the way it went—
                          I stepped back, and I turned around,
And I walked down through the rhododendron
And never looked back,
                  truly awake in the throbbing world,
And I ducked through the low flap
Of the tent, so quietly, and I went to sleep
And never told anyone
Till years later when I thought I knew what it meant,
                                    which now I've forgot.

——————

And this one is questionable,
Though sworn to me by an old friend
Who'd killed a six-foot diamondback about seven o'clock in the
        morning

(He'd found it coiled in a sunny place),
And threw it into a croker sack with its head chopped off,
                              and threw the sack in the back of a jeep,
Then left for his day's work
On the farm.
                    That evening he started to show the snake
To someone, and put his hand in the sack to pull it out.
As he reached in, the snake's stump struck him.
His wrist was bruised for a week.

———————

It's not age,
              nor time with its gold eyelid and blink,
Nor dissolution in all its mimicry
That lifts us and sorts us out.
It's discontinuity
                and all its spangled coming between
That sends us apart and keeps us there in a dread.
It's what's in the rearview mirror,
                              smaller and out of sight.

———————

What do you do when the words don't come to you anymore,
And all the embolisms fade in the dirt?
And the ocean sings in its hammock,
                              rocking itself back and forth?
And you live at the end of the road where the sky starts its dark
    decline?

The barking goes on and on
                      from the far hill, constantly
Sticking its noise in my good ear.

Goodbye, Miss Sweeney, goodbye.
I'm starting to think about the psychotransference of all things.
It's small bones in the next life.
It's small bones,
              and heel and toe forever and ever.

The Other Side of the River

Easter again, and a small rain falls
On the mockingbird and the housefly,
                              on the Chevrolet
In its purple joy
And the TV antennas huddled across the hillside—

Easter again, and the palm trees hunch
Deeper beneath their burden,
                              the dark puddles take in
Whatever is given them,
And nothing rises more than halfway out of itself—

Easter with all its little mouths open into the rain.

———————

There is no metaphor for the spring's disgrace,
No matter how much the rose leaves look like bronze dove hearts,
No matter how much the plum trees preen in the wind.

For weeks I've thought about the Savannah River,
For no reason,
                  and the winter fields around Garnett, South Carolina,
My brother and I used to hunt
At Christmas,
                  Princess and Buddy working the millet stands
And the vine-lipped face of the pine woods
In their languorous zigzags,
The quail, when they flushed, bursting like shrapnel points
Between the trees and the leggy shrubs
                              into the undergrowth,

Everything else in motion as though under water,
My brother and I, the guns, their reports tolling from far away
Through the aqueous, limb-filtered light,
December sun like a single tropical fish
Uninterested anyway,
                     suspended and holding still
In the coral stems of the pearl-dusked and distant trees . . .

There is no metaphor for any of this,
Or the meta-weather of April,
The vinca blossoms like deep bruises among the green.

It's linkage I'm talking about,
                     and harmonies and structures
And all the various things that lock our wrists to the past.

Something infinite behind everything appears,
                         and then disappears.

It's all a matter of how
                  you narrow the surfaces.
It's all a matter of how you fit in the sky.

Often, at night, when the stars seem as close as they do now, and as
       full,
And the trees balloon and subside in the way they do
                         when the wind is right,
As they do now after the rain,
                  the sea way off with its false sheen,
And the sky that slick black of wet rubber,
I'm fifteen again, and back on Mount Anne in North Carolina
Repairing the fire tower,
Nobody else around but the horse I packed in with,
                       and five days to finish the job.

Those nights were the longest nights I ever remember,
The lake and pavilion 3,000 feet below
                              as though modeled in tinfoil,
And even more distant than that,
The last fire out, the after-reflection of Lake Llewellyn
Aluminum glare in the sponged dark,
Lightning bugs everywhere,
                              the plump stars
Dangling and falling near on their black strings.

These nights are like that,
The silvery alphabet of the sea
                              increasingly difficult to transcribe,
And larger each year, everything farther away, and less clear,
Than I want it to be,
                              not enough time to do the job,
And faint thunks in the earth,
As though somewhere nearby a horse was nervously pawing the
      ground.

                    ————

I want to sit by the bank of the river,
                    in the shade of the evergreen tree,
And look in the face of whatever,
                    the whatever that's waiting for me.

                    ————

There comes a point when everything starts to dust away
More quickly than it appears,
                              when what we have to comfort the dark
Is just that dust, and just its going away.

Twenty-five years ago I used to sit on this jut of rocks
As the sun went down like an offering through the glaze
And backfires of Monterey Bay,
And anything I could think of was mine because it was there

                              in front of me, numinously everywhere,
Appearing and piling up . . .

So to have come to this,
                    remembering what I did do, and what I didn't do,
The gulls whimpering over the boathouse,
                              the monarch butterflies
Cruising the flower beds,
And all the soft hairs of spring thrusting up through the wind,
And the sun, as it always does,
                    dropping into its slot without a click,
Is a short life of trouble.

Homage to Claude Lorrain

I had a picture by him—a print, I think—on my bedroom wall
In Verona in 1959,
                    via Anzani n. 3.
Or maybe a drawing, a rigged ship in a huge sea,
Storm waves like flames above my bed.
It's lost between there and here now,
                              and has been for years,
Trapped in the past's foliage, as so much else is
In spite of our constancy, or how
We rattle the branches and keep our lights on the right place.

The room had a vaulted ceiling and faced east.
The living room was a tower with skylights on four sides.
A third room sloped with the roof
                          until it was two feet high at the far wall,
All of this part of a reconstructed attic, and washed white.

I lived there for two years,
                    one block from the Adige
Where seagulls, like little loaves of fresh bread,
Drifted and turned on its grey coils.
Between the sea fires of Claude Lorrain
                          and the curled sheets of the river,
I burned on my swivel stool
Night after night,
                looking into the future, its charred edges
Holding my life like a frame
I'd hope to fit into one day, unsigned and rigged for the deeps.

Mantova

Mantegna on all the walls,
The Mincio puddled outside the gates,
                                        clouds tattooed on its blue chest,
Mantova floats in the pigeon-light of late afternoon
Twenty-two years ago.
Rain shoots its white cuffs across the scene.

I remember a dream I had once in Mantova,
Everyone in it in full dress,
                        refectory hall,
Goblets and white linen.
At the near end of the table, heaped on a bronze salver
Like quail, all wishbone and delicate leg,
The roast children were served up.
                                "You must try the thighs,"
My host said, his gloves still on.
                                "You must try the thighs."

Half the sky full of rain, and half not,
Reeds under water pressure to stay still,
The river oncoming but not flashed,
Everything upside down,
                        the sky at rest underfoot.
Words, but who can remember?

What words does the sky know, or the clouds know?

On the wall of the summer house,
                        where Giulio Romano left him,
The lion sips at the riverbank, and the trees provide.

Driving to Passalacqua, 1960

The road is a hard road,
                         and the river is wadded and flattened out
Due west of Santa Maria dell'Ortolo.
Each morning I drove with its steady breathing right to my right,
Dawn like a courtier
With his high white hat just coming into the room,
Ponte Pietra cut in the morning gauze,
                                Catullus off to my left
Released in the labials of the sunlight,
Fire on the water,
                daylight striking its match
Wherever it pleased
Along the Adige and stitched cross-tiles of San Fermo . . .

What do I do with all this?
                     Phlegethon
He must have crossed,
                Dante, I mean,
His cloak like a net as he glided and stepped over the stones.
I hurry on by, breakfast
In mind, and the day's duty, half-left at the *bivio*.
Our outfit was out in town,
                     in hiding, spiked fence and three Chevrolets
In front when I pulled up for roll call
And the morning mail and settling in,
DiCenzo signed out for Udine, and Joe for Vienna.
All day the river burned by my desk
                as I sailed my boats down its licks for a foot or so.

Three Poems of Departure

1

Sitting again on the front porch of the first cabin.
Grind of the deerfly, hone of the bee.
Someone is mourning inconsolably somewhere else.
Yellow of goldenrod, bronze of the grass.
By the creek bridge, the aspen leaves are waving goodbye, goodbye.
Silence of paintbrush and cow pink.
Take the dirt from the old trail up in your hand, Pilgrim,
                                    and throw it into the wind.

2

The meadow surrounds us on three sides,
Steep woods to the north;
It's fifty-one miles downriver to where the highway begins.
I leave by the opposite way,
                    over the summit
Through deadfall and clear cut and shell-shot snow of July.

Already sundown has passed you and follows me up the road,
Color of dragonfly wings.
On the other side, as I start down,
                            it passes me too,
Your voice now flat as a handkerchief
Folded away for miles in its pine drawer.

3

28 August and first frost
Like a horizon across the meadow.
                              The yellow top
Of the signal tamarack
Sticks up like a stalk of goldenrod from the southern mountain,
Autumn starting to pull in its heavy net.

Thistle spores tumble like star-webs between the trees.
The slough grass is brown in the dry channels.
Tomorrow we leave for the desert,
                                almost two thousand miles away.
But tonight, under the white eye of Betelgeuse,
We'll point out the pony stars, and their gusty hooves.

Italian Days

1

Thinking again of a weekend trip to Ferrara,
Cosimo Tura on one wall,
                              Miss d'Este long gone from the next,
I took from Verona once,
A place where the streets were as wide as Parisian boulevards,
The Po like a frayed rope out past the bulge of the dikes.

The weekend before I'd been to Merano and back,
And almost become a squib
                              in the *Stars & Stripes*
When the helicopter's engine stopped
Thousands of feet above the Brenner highway,
And we began to slide sideways down the air
As quietly as a snowflake,
                              the huge rotary blades above us
Circling like paddle churns in the wind

Languidly,
            the stillness abrupt, the plane
In a long slip like a scimitar curve toward the ground
Rising to meet us, its trees
Focusing automatically larger with each look
As though raised through a microscope,
The engine catching at last on its last turn,
Pine branches less than fifty feet below us,
                              the blade-slide bottoming out

As we started to rise and swing north
Up the Val d'Adige and into the emerald sundown
Outside Merano . . .
                              Back up out of darkness an hour later,
The houses beginning to flash on like matches below,
Left over Trento and left over Schio
                              and down, everyone out to supper,
The waitress admonishing Manzolin, "*Non si taglia la pasta.*"

Cut to Ferrara, and me
Threading my way out of town through bicycles, Vespas and runty
        Fiats
South to Ravenna and Rimini,
                              the lap of the Adriatic
And western Byzantium
In the long grasses of S. Apollinare in Classe,
The field stubble gold in the noon sun.

Cut to Verona, the town I always left from,
Work over, and Happy Hour,
                              Modugno on every phonograph
On Via Mazzini, "*Ciao, ciao, bambina . . .*"
It's 1959 and after supper,
Everyone disappearing like rain
From the streets and Caffè Dante, the fog in,
Can Grande skulking and disappearing in marble above his tomb

As I do along the cobblestones
He grins down on,
                              gone through the fog toward S. Anastasia
And the Due Torri, everything swaddled as though in newsprint,
The river off to the right like a licking sound,
Up past the Duomo,
                              then right and across the last bridge,
Where the beggar loomed in her burning chair.
Each night as I passed her
                              it took a hundred lire to put out the fire.

Up north, in the watersheds and rock slides of the Dolomites,
Snow has been leaving its same message
For thousands of years
                    on the bark of the cedar trees.
There is no stopping the comings and goings in this world,
No stopping them, to and fro.

2

Palladio's buildings shone like the collar on someone's dog
In Vicenza, the only inscript in all the town.
For the rest, it was Goldstein patrolling the avenues
At sundown with hot hands.
                    And Venezia, Lord of the Bees,
In the dark hives of the Hotel Artù with hot hands.
It was Charles with hot hands,
His fingers on this and that wherever he turned
In the bars of Little America.
It was weekend and off-duty and kicking the gong
In a foreign country,
                    left foot and right foot.

Sister water, brother fire, gentle my way
Across,
        one foot on the river, one foot in the flames,
My lack of ability to remember it right.
The time we spotted the Vicentine,
For instance, it rained and dimpled all the way back,
With Grace in his lap and him driving,
Sneezing and making amends.
On alternate Sundays we'd drive to Soave and Asolo,
Padova and the Euganean Hills,
Always looking for the event,
                    not knowing that we were it.

This was the world we lived in,
And couldn't get shut of.
                    And these were the rocks we walked on,
Milano, Certosa, footstep
                    after footstep echoing down the galleries,
Goldstein checking the nuns out,
Venezia settling like smoke at the unbitten center of things.
One Sunday after the Trattoria La Brera,
We went to Scuderi's place, his huge canvases
Stacked like Sheetrock against the wall.
                              "I have to keep them like this,"
He said, "to keep my life in order."
He died the next winter,
                    the heater electrocuting him in the bathtub.

Some nights, when the stars flash their gang codes,
And the fog slides in as cautiously as a bride
Across the steps the trees make
                    up from the sea,
And the gnatlight starts to solidify
Like a crust on the palm leaf and the pepper switch,
And the smell of the paper-whites
                    hangs like a June garden
Above the kitchen table,
Scuderi calls out my name
                    as I climb the six flights to his room
And stand in the doorway again,
Electric and redivivus in the world of light

He lived in inside his paintings for all those years,
Vaseline light
                    through the slow filter of late November,
Acid light off the north Italian lakes,
Shorthand of light from the olive leaves
                              as they turn and tick in the wind,
Last light of the *dopoguerra* lifting Milan like a ship

In the Lombardy night outside his window
On top of the city wall,
                            bar light and aftermath,
Scuderi whitening to grain-out and then to blank,
Light like a sheet of paper
Everywhere, flat and unwrinkled and unreturnable.

        3

At the end of the last word,
When night comes walking across the lake on its hands,
And nothing appears in the mirror,
                                    or has turned to water
Where nothing walks or lies down,
What will your question be,
Whistling the dogs of mold in, giving them meat?
And what will it profit you?

No thought of that back then,
Bivouacked outside the castle above Marostica
Whose walls
            downswept and pinioned the town like wings
In its coming-to-rest,
                        the town square
Blocked out like a chessboard black and white,
Black and white from up there,
Where the rook looked down on the knight's play.

What eschatology of desire
                            could move us in those days,
What new episiotomy of the word?
At San Gimignano, outside of town,
I did see that no one could last for good,
That no one could answer back from the other side.
Still, I'd like to think I've learned how to speak to them,

I'd like to think I know how to conjugate
                              "Can you hear me?" and "What?"

In Rome, on the Via Cassia,
                              there was opportunity enough
For that in the catacombs,
                              the lost bodies slipped in their slots
Like letters someone had never answered,
And then tossed out,
A chance to step back from the light
                              of the strung electric bulb,
And ask again if our first day in the dark
Is our comfort or signature.

Most of what I remember
Has nothing to do with any of that, it turns out:
A view from the Pinacoteca window across Siena
One morning in 1959
                    and out to the hillscapes and olive shine;
The way Piero della Francesca's *Madonna del Parto*
Was leaning against the wall
                              in Monterchi, and still unlit;
The eel fisherman that May twilight along the Mincio River.

But Scuderi did, and the helicopter did,
And the full moon like Borso's skull on the Zattere,
Fog smoking up from the humped lagoon;
                              and Eve coming out of Adam's rib
On San Zeno's doors in Verona,
                              her foot still stuck in his side;
And the morning we sat on the terrace,
                              Jim Gates and Tom Fucile and I,
In Bassano, the bowler of Monte Grappa across the valley,
Ghost hat on the head of northern Italy.

There is, in the orchards of Sommacampagna,
A sleet-like and tenuous iridescence that falls

Through the peach trees whenever it rains.
                              The blossoms parachute to the ground
So heavy and so distinct,
And the light above Riva spokes out from under the clouds
Like Blake,
              the wires for the grapevines beading their little rainbows,
The cars planing by on the highway,
                              shooshing their golden plumes . . .

What gifts there are are all here, in this world.

Three Poems for the New Year

1

I have nothing to say about the way the sky tilts
Toward the absolute,
                        or why I live at the edge
Of the black boundary,
                        a continent where the waves
Counsel my coming in and my going out.

I have nothing to say about the brightness and drear
Of any of that, or the vanity
                        of our separate consolations.
I have nothing to say about the companies of held breath.

All year I have sung in vain,
Like a face breaking up in the font of holy water,
                        not hungry, not pure of heart.
All year as my body, sweet pilgrimage,
                        moved from the dark to the dark.

What true advice the cicada leaves.

2

How strange it is to awake
Into middle age, Rimbaud left blue and out cold
In the snow,
                the Alps wriggling away to a line

In the near distance,
                      someone you don't know
Coming to get your body, revive it, and arrange for the train.

How strange to awake to that,

The windows all fogged with breath,
The landscape outside in a flash,
                              and gone like a scarf
On the neck of someone else,
                        so white, so immaculate,
The deserts and caravans
Hanging like Christmas birds in the ice-dangled evergreens.

   3

All day at the window seat
                       looking out, the red knots
Of winter hibiscus deep in the foregreen,
Slick globes of oranges in the next yard,
Many oranges,
               and slow winks in the lemon trees
Down the street, slow winks when the wind blows the leaves back.

The ache for fame is a thick dust and weariness in the heart.

All day with the knuckle of solitude
To gnaw on,
              the turkey buzzards and red-tailed hawk
Lifting and widening concentrically over the field,
Brush-tails of the pepper branches
                              writing invisibly on the sky . . .

The ache for anything is a thick dust in the heart.

Roma I

To start with, it looked abstract
                            that first year from the balcony
Over the Via del Babuino,
Local color as far as the eye could see,
                            and mumbled in slaps and clumps
Of gouaches constantly to itself,
A gentian snood of twilight in winter,
                            blood orange in spring,
And ten thousand yards of glass in the summer sky.
Wherever you looked in October, the night was jigged.

(In front of the Ristorante Bolognese,
Monica Vitti and Michelangelo Antonioni are having an aperitif,
Watched by a hundred people.
                            On the marble plaque
On the building across the street from my room to the Polish patriot
Whose name escapes me forever,
The words start to disappear in the April nightswell.
The river of cars turns its small lights on,
                            and everyone keeps on looking at everyone else.)

Rome in Rome? We're all leading afterlives
                            of one sort or another,
Wrapped in bird feathers, pecking away at our gathered seed,
The form inside the form inside.
And nothing's more common by now than the obelisk
At one end of the street
                            and the stone boat at the other . . .
The smell of a dozen dinners is borne up
On exhaust fumes,
                    timeless, somehow, and vaguely reassuring.

Roma II

I looked long and long at my mother's miniature
The next year,
          the year I lived on the east side
Of the church building that overlooked the Campo dei Fiori.
Her body had entered the oak grove.
By the river of five-sided leaves she had laid it down,
Hummingbird hard at the yellow shells of the sour grass,
Red throat in the light vouchsafed,
          then quick hum to a marigold.

The poem is a self-portrait
          always, no matter what mask
You take off and put back on.
As this one is, color of cream and a mouthful of air.
Rome is like that, and we are,
          taken off and put back on.
Downstairs, in front of the *Pollarolla*,
The Irish poets are sketching themselves in,
          and the blue awnings, and motorbikes.
They draw till we're all in, even our hands.

Surely, as has been said, emptiness is the beginning of all things.
Thus wind over water,
          thus tide-pull and sand-sheen
When the sea turns its lips back . . .
Still, we stand by the tree whose limbs branch out like bones,
Or steps in the bronchial sediment.
And the masters stand in their azure gowns,
Sticks in their hands, palm leaves like birds above their heads.

97)

Homage to Cesare Pavese

Death will come and it will have your eyes
From morning to morning, sleepless,
                              an old remorse.
Your eyes will be vain words, a silence
You'll see as you lean out to the mirror
Each day,
            the one look that it has for everyone.

It will be like ooze from the sea,
Like stopping a vice
                    and the sin. It will be like stopping the sin.
It will be the dead face in the mirror
Listening to shut lips.
It will descend silently,
                      speechlessly into whirlpools.

Death will come and it will have your eyes,
Ridiculous vice
            and the same look.
You are the great weariness.
You are scorched and burned back by the sea.
You say nothing,
            and nobody speaks to you.

This is a balance sheet and the names don't count.
One nail on top of another,
                        four nails make a cross.
Nothing can add to the past—
Woman is as woman does,
                    and night is always the night.
With its black heart and its black hands it lays me down.

Cryopexy

Looming and phosphorescent against the dark,
Words, always words.
                     What language does light speak?
Vowels hang down from the pepper tree
                             in their green and their gold.

The star charts and galactic blood trails behind the eye
Where the lights are, and the links and chains are,
                           cut wall through ascending wall,
Indigo corridors, the intolerable shine
                       transgressing heaven's borders . . .

What are the colors of true splendor,
                        yellow and white,
Carnation and ivory, petal and bone?
Everything comes from fire.

Glare and glare-white,
                   light like a plate of isinglass
Under the lid,
             currents of fox-fire between the layers,
And black dots like the blood bees of Paradise . . .

Radiance comes through the eye
                    and lodges like cut glass in the mind,
Never vice versa,
Somatic and self-contained.

————

Like soiled stars from the night-blooming jasmine vine
Espaliered against the sky,
                    char flakes rise from their blank deeps
Through peach light and apricot
Into the endlessness behind the eye.

————

Blood clots, like numb houseflies, hang
In the alabaster and tracery,
                    icy detritus
Rocked in the swish and tug
                    of the eye's twice-turned and moonless tides.
Behind them, tourmaline thread-ladders
Web up through the nothingness,
                    the diamond and infinite glare . . .

————

Weightlessness underwrites everything
In the deep space of the eye,
                    the wash and drift of oblivion
Sifting the color out,
                    polishing, still polishing
Long after translucence comes.

————

One black, electric blot, blood-blown,
Vanishes like Eurydice
                    away from the light's mouth

And under the vitreous bulge of the eye's hill,
Down, O down, down . . .

————————

Clocking the slurs and backlit snow
In their dark descent:
A Vaseline-colored medicine cloud floats to the left,
A comet-like shadow-slur floats to the right
Through a different throb,
                                the snow in its quartzed downfall.

————————

Sometimes, in the saffron undercurrents
                                trailing like Buddhist prayer robes
Across the eye,
                clear eels and anemones
Bob and circle and sink back through the folds,
Caught in the sleeve of the curl's turn.

————————

Across the eye's Pacific, stars
                                drop in the black water like pursed lips,
Islands and tiny boats
Dipping under the white lid of the strung horizon,
                                this one in amethyst, this one in flame.

T'ang Notebook

Fine clouds open their outfits
                                and show us their buttons.
Moonlight widens the waves.
Step on your own song and listen to mine,
Not bitter like yours,
                        not flicked raw by lashes of dust.
Already, over Italy, the cold sun rises.

————

How I would like a mountain
                                if I had means enough to live as a recluse.
I would like to renounce it all
And turn toward the ash-gold of flame
                                mullioned between the palm fronds.

————

That constellation, with its seven high stars,
                                is lifting its sword in the midnight.
I love you, dog, I love you.

————

Remain here and lengthen your days,
                                Pilgrim,
Fame is a mist of grief on the river waves . . .

————

The low, wet clouds move faster than you do,
Snowed moon, your jade hair sleet
                                and grown thin.
All night I ask what time it is.

———

Stories of passion make sweet dust . . .
Sunset like a girl's robe falling away long ago . . .
An old song handles my heart . . .

———

Outside the side door, a luck-spider
                              huge in the flashlight's lamp,
Rappels down the air
                    to single a stitch and make her starred bed.
In the dark past the hemlock, something with small, bright wings
Has come from a great distance, and is tired
                              and wants to lie down.

———

Night spreads its handful of star-clusters and one eclipse
Above the palm tree.
There are shuddering birds and dead grasses
Wherever I turn my face.

———

The ten thousand starfish caught in the net of heaven
Flash at the sky's end.
Gulls settle, like grains of dust, on the black sand.
Lady of Light, Donna Dolorosa,
                         you drift like a skeleton
Through the night clouds.
The surf comes in and goes out like smoke.
Give me a sign,
              show me the blessing pierced in my side.

———

This wind that comes in off the Pacific,
Where the color of mountains both is and is not,
                         ripples the distant marsh grass
And the grey doors of the sea.

The evening begins to close like a morning glory.
Like fear in a little boat,
                              the light slips under the sky.

———————

When the mind is loosened and borne up,
The body is lightened
                    and feels it too could float in the wind,
A bell-sound between here and sleep.

———————

A water egret planes down like a page of blank paper
Toward the edge of the noon sky.
                    Let me, like him, find an island of white reeds
To settle down on, under the wind, forgetting words.

Arkansas Traveller

On the far side of the water, high on a sandbar,
Grandfathers are lolling above the Arkansas River,
Guitars in their laps, cloth caps like Cagney down over their eyes.
A woman is strumming a banjo.
                              Another adjusts her bow tie
And boiled shirtwaist.
And in the half-light the frogs begin from their sleep
To ascend into darkness,
Vespers recalibrate through the underbrush,
                              the insect choir
Offering its clear soprano
Out of the vaulted gum trees into the stained glass of the sky.

––––––––––

Almost ninety-five years to the day I saw
Ellison Smythe passed out
                    on the back seat of an Oldsmobile 88
In the spring of 1952 in Biltmore Forest, N.C.,
Who then rose up from the dark of his sixteenth year
And said to the nothingness:
                    Where are we,
Who's driving this goddamn thing?
My great-grandfather stepped off the boat
                    from the archduchy of Upper Austria
And headed north to the territory.
And into another war
                    here, just past the Mississippi,
On the Arkansas.
            I don't know that it was such a great blessing
Sending us to Arkansas,

But it was so regarded at the time, and we're grateful to Gen. Jackson.
Still, don't let me die as Grandmother did,
                                    suddenly on a steamboat
Stuck fast on a sandbar unable to get to Little Rock.
And was four years later a volunteer captain
In the Confederacy,
                    and took a Minie ball in his palate
At Chickamauga he carried there till his death
Almost half a century afterward.
                                And wrote a poem back
To the widow of one of his men about a sure return
"Where life is not a breath,
Nor life's affections, transient fire . . . in heaven's light."
And was captured again,
                        and wounded again, confined for two years
At Rock Island prison.
And came back to Little Rock and *began his career.*
And died at sixty-six,
                    a ticket to Cuba stored flat in his jacket pocket.

When Jesus walked on the night grass
                                they say not even the dew trembled.
Such intricate catechisms of desire.
Such golden cars down the wrong side of the sky.

Each summer in Little Rock,
                        like a monk in his cell
Saying the lesson over and over
Until it is shining, all day I'd prove up my childhood till lights-out
Snapped on the fireflies that floated
Like miniature jellyfish
                        off the reefs of the sleeping porch
Whose jasmine-and-rose-scented air broke over me back and forth
Before I could count the half of them,
                                and settled me under.

This was before I was ten.
That year my grandfather, my look-alike on the sandbar, died,
The war ended, and nothing was ever the same way
Again.
        His mantelpiece clock sits on my dresser now,
Still gilded and nineteenth-century.
Devotion, remember, is what counts.
Without it you're exiled, twisted and small.

————————

The next morning we'd play golf,
                        four holes on the back side,
Trailing our footprints like paired bodies emptied and left out to dry
In the web of sunlight and wet grass
                        behind us over the clipped fairways,
My grandmother and I up before anyone else
Each day I was there,
                the sun already a huge, hot thumb
At seven o'clock on our bare heads.
Later, its print still warm on my forehead,
Sunset like carrot juice down the left pane of the sky
Into the indeterminacy of somewhere else,
I'd roll the tarpaulin down and up
On the sleeping porch,
                the frog-shrill and the insect-shrill
Threading out of the bushes
                as palpable as a heartstring,
Whatever that was back then, always in memory . . .

————————

To speak of the dead is to make them live again:
                        we invent what we need.
Knot by knot I untie myself from the past
And let it rise away from me like a balloon.
What a small thing it becomes.
What a bright tweak at the vanishing point, blue on blue.

To Giacomo Leopardi in the Sky

If you are become an eternal idea,
Refusing investiture in our pink rags,

                                                 wise beyond body and form,
Or if you housel elsewhere a different sun
In one of the other aethers,

                            from down here
Where our years are fanged and omnivorous,
Listen to what these words say, from one who remembers you.

––––––––––

July 17th, on the front deck
Looking out through the slats and palm leaves,
The ocean horizonless and sending out signals,
I start to unmarble

                            interminable spaces beyond it,
Silences so immense they sound like wind,
Like this wind that dismays me
With its calm

                            as it pulls the sheet of the night
Over my head.
How sweet it is to drown in such sure water.

––––––––––

Whenever I see you
On your left side through the clouds
Looking down on us,

                            our tongues tied, our friends all gone,
Our hearts and breaths with the air let out of them,
You make me bitter for being so much like you.

What day did I take this picture you have no part in?
1959, no leaves on the trees, late fall.
                        Ponte Pietra over the Adige.
Verona, early morning.
What purpose your brief drifting along my course?
You try to erase your tracks
                    but you're too far from the ground.
You've throbbed enough.
Everything on the earth is worth your sighs.

———————

Never to see the light is best, you say,
                        who were made for joy,
Your neck of chalk like a vapor trail across the sky.

———————

I know you're up there, hiding behind the noon light
And the crystal of space.
                Down here,
In the lurch and gasp the day makes as it waits for you
In your black suit and mother-of-pearl,
The mail comes, the garbage goes,
                        the paired butterflies
Dip and swoop in formation,
Bees trail their tongues
                    and tiptoe around the circumferences
Of the melaleuca puffs,
Sucking the sweetness up, July 27th,
The hummingbird asleep on her branch,
                        the spider drawn up in flame.

———————

You kept reading and reading,
Vowel over consonant
                then three steps to the stars,

109)

And there you languish,
                              outlined in flash points and solid geometry,
Epistle in tatters . . .

You doom us who see your face.
You force on us your sorrow:
So frail and vile throughout,
                              as ours is,
It assails the ear like paradise.
The moon goes up and goes down,
                              roused and quenched low.
You bend like a calling card away from the dawn.
You doom us who see your face.

It's the mind, not the body,
That bears us up and shines a light in our eyes:
If spirit is nothingness,
                    I'd rather the light came back than the light came on.

Noon, and you're there again on the other side of the sky.
Two kites have nested in the dry skirt
Of the palm tree
                    and scrape their voices like fingernails
Against the windowpane of the air
When they flutter down, quick fingers, to feed their chicks.
You'd like it on this side, I think.
                              Summer is everywhere, your favorite,
And dirt still crumbles and falls like small rain from the hand.
The wind blows in from the sea.
The girls are pretty and everyone is sad.

The night is clear and incised,
The moon like a gold record
                    above the houses and avocado grove,
And you're back,
                    floating behind the star's stitching,
Such fine thread to sip through.
Do you remember the pain of the way it was for you,
Teresa's song scratching the scab off your own youth
And approaching end,
The days not long enough, and the nights not long enough
For you to suffer it all?
                    You'd do the same again, I'll bet,
And live the same life,
Paper umbrella above your head
To keep the snow off,
                    the color of snowfall like curtains across your eyes.

Not one word has ever melted in glory not one.
We keep on sending them up, however,
As the sun rains down.
                    You did it yourself,
All those nights looking up at the sky, wanting to be there
Away from the grief of being here
In the wrong flesh.
They must look funny to you now,
Rising like smoke signals into the infinite,
The same letter over and over,
                    big o and little o.

August 15th, and ten days
And 1,700 miles from where we last spoke, less than a twitch
For you,
                    seventy years into the past for me
As the crow flies and the weather burns.
And even here, like the hand of a drowning man, your own hand

Points out from behind the stars
                              still without urgency
The Bear and the dark waters
Each boat of flesh sets sail on . . .
Such hurt, and I turn the page
                              to this place, built in 1912
By someone who'd never heard your name
But knew your face on clear nights
                              over Mount Caribou
As you wheeled west, your mouth full of stars.

———————

That's all I wanted to say.
Think of me now and then, as I think of you
When the moon's like a golden tick on the summer sky
Gorged with light:
                              you're part of my parts of speech.
Think of me now and then. I'll think of you.

Looking at Pictures

How many times have I come here
                            to look at these photographs
And reproductions of all I've thought most beautiful
In the natural world,
And tried to enter the tired bodies assembled in miniature?

St. Francis, for instance, who saw the fire in the pig's mouth,
And trees full of the drowned
                            who forgot to cross themselves.
Or the last half-page of the Verse of Light in Arabic
                                        torn from the Koran,
Tacked like a terrible crystal this side of the reading lamp.
Beside it Adam and Eve in agony
Are ushered out through the stone gates of Paradise.

On the other side of the room
A Fra Angelico angel beats time on a tambourine:
Everything's music to his ears.
                        And Rothko has a black-on-red
Painting below it I'd sink through flat on my back
Endlessly down into nothingness . . .

But not now. Not now when the hound of the Pope's men
Is leaping, not now
                        when the banner of St. George
Dragontails out of the sky. Not now
When our fathers stand in their riding boots, arms crossed,
Trying to tell us something we can't quite hear,
                            our ears jugged like Kafka's.

The devil eats us, I know, but our arms don't touch his neck.
Help me remember, Madonna of Tenderness,
                              that everything slides away
Into him stealthily.

St. Francis is feeding the birds again.
And someone with wings and brown hair
                              is telling Mary something
Again in a different dress.

St. Anne and Château Noir,
The flute player from 2200 B.C.
Out of the Cyclades—St. Ignatius Loyola
                              would find no rope in all this
To cinch around himself. It's synaptical here,
And rearranged.

We stare at the backs of our own heads continually
Walking in cadence into the past,
Great-grandfathers before their suicides,
                              Venice in sunshine, Venice in rain,
Someone standing in front of the sea
                              watching the waves come in . . .

California Dreaming

We are not born yet, and everything's crystal under our feet.
We are not brethren, we are not underlings.
We are another nation,
                              living by voices that you will never hear,
Caught in the net of splendor
                              of time-to-come on the earth.
We shine in our distant chambers, we are golden.

————————

Midmorning, and Darvon dustfall off the Pacific
Stuns us to ecstasy,
                              October sun
Stuck like a tack on the eastern drift of the sky,
The idea of God on the other,
                              body by body
Rinsed in the Sunday prayer-light, draining away
Into the undercoating and slow sparks of the west,
                              which is our solitude and our joy.

————————

I've looked at this ridge of lights for six years now
                              and still don't like it,
Strung out like Good Friday along a cliff
That Easters down to the ocean,
A dark wing with ruffled feathers as far out as Catalina
Fallen from some sky,
                              ruffled and laid back by the wind,
Santa Ana that lisps its hot breath
                              on the neck of everything.

What if the soul indeed is outside the body,

                                    a little rainfall of light

Moistening our every step, prismatic, apotheosizic?

What if inside the body another shape is waiting to come out,

White as a quilt, loose as a fever,

                                 and sways in the easy tides there?

What other anagoge in this life but the self?

What other ladder to Paradise

                        but the smooth handholds of the rib cage?

High in the palm tree the orioles twitter and grieve.

We twitter and grieve, the spider twirls the honey bee,

Who twitters and grieves, around in her net,

                               then draws it by one leg

Up to the fishbone fern leaves inside the pepper tree

                                  swaddled in silk

And turns it again and again until it is shining.

Some nights, when the rock-and-roll band next door has quit playing,

And the last helicopter has thwonked back to the Marine base,

And the dark lets all its weight down

                           to within a half inch of the ground,

I sit outside in the gold lamé of the moon

                     as the town sleeps and the country sleeps

Like flung confetti around me,

And wonder just what in the hell I'm doing out here

So many thousands of miles away from what I know best.

And what I know best

                   has nothing to do with Point Conception

And Avalon and the long erasure of ocean

Out there where the landscape ends.

What I know best is a little thing.

It sits on the far side of the simile,

                     the like that's like the like.

———————

Today is sweet stuff on the tongue.
The question of how we should live our lives in this world
Will find no answer from us
                              this morning,
Sunflick, the ocean humping its back
Beneath us, shivering out
                              wave after wave we fall from
And cut through in a white scar of healed waters,
Our wet suits glossed slick as seals,
                              our boards grown sharp as cries.
We rise and fall like the sun.

———————

Ghost of the Muse and her dogsbody
Suspended above the beach, November 25th,
Sun like a Valium disc, smog like rust in the trees.
White-hooded and friar-backed,
                              a gull choir eyeballs the wave reach.
Invisibly pistoned, the sea keeps it up,
                              plunges and draws back, plunges and draws back,
Yesterday hung like a porcelain cup behind the eyes,
Sonorous valves, insistent extremities,
                              the worm creeping out of the heart . . .

———————

Who are these people we pretend to be,
                              untouched by the setting sun?
They stand less stiffly than we do, and handsomer,
First on the left foot, and then the right.
Just for a moment we see ourselves inside them,
                              peering out,
And then they go their own way and we go ours,
Back to the window seat above the driveway,
Christmas lights in the pepper tree,
                              black Madonna

117)

Gazing out from the ailanthus.
Chalk eyes downcast, heavy with weeping and bitterness,
Her time has come round again.

————————

Piece by small piece the world falls away from us like spores
From a milkweed pod,
     and everything we have known,
And everyone we have known,
Is taken away by the wind to forgetfulness,
Somebody always humming,
      California dreaming . . .

ZONE

JOURNALS

(1988)

Yard Journal

—Mist in the trees, and soiled water and grass cuttings splotch
The driveway,
                  afternoon starting to bulk up in the west
A couple of hours down the road:
Strange how the light hubs out and wheels
                                concentrically back and forth
After a rain, as though the seen world
Quavered inside a water bead
                    swung from a grass blade:
The past is never the past:
                  it lies like a long tongue
We walk down into the moist mouth of the future, where new teeth
Nod like new stars around us,
And winds that itch us, and plague our ears,
                      sound curiously like the old songs.

—Deep dusk and lightning bugs
                  alphabetize on the east wall,
The carapace of the sky blue-ribbed and buzzing
Somehow outside it all,
Trees dissolving against the night's job,
                  houses melting in air:
Somewhere out there an image is biding its time,
Burning like Abraham in the cold, swept
                  expanses of heaven,
Waiting to take me in and complete my equation:
What matters is abstract, and is what love is,
Candescent inside the memory,
                continuous
And unexpungable, as love is . . .

—Blue jay's bound like a kangaroo's in the lawn's high grass,
Then up in a brushstroke
                              and over the hedge in one arc.
Light weights down the azalea plants,
Yesterday's cloud banks enfrescoed still
                                        just under the sky's cornice,
Cardinal quick transfusion into the green arm of the afternoon.
Wax-like flowers of sunlight drift
                              through the dwarf orchard and float
Under the pygmied peaches and pears
All over America,
                    and here, too, the blossoms
Continuing down from nowhere, out of the blue.
The mockingbird's shadow is burned in the red clay below him.

—Exclusion's the secret: what's missing is what appears
Most visible to the eye:
                        the more luminous anything is,
The more it subtracts what's around it,
Peeling away the burned skin of the world
                                        making the unseen seen:
Body by new body they all rise into the light
Tactile and still damp,
That rhododendron and dogwood tree, that spruce,
An architecture of absence,
                              a landscape whose words
Are imprints, dissolving images after the eyelids close:
I take them away to keep them there—
                              that hedgehorn, for instance, that stalk . . .

—A bumblebee the size of my thumb
                              rises like Geryon
From the hard Dantescan gloom
Under my window sash to lip the rain gutter's tin *bolgia*,
Then backs out like a hummingbird
                              spiraling languidly out of sight,
Shoulders I've wanted to sit on, a ride I've wanted to take,

Deposited into the underlight
                              of cities thronged in the grass,
Fitful illuminations, iron-colored plain that lies
Littered with music and low fires,
                              stone edge of the pit
At the end of every road,
First faces starting to swim up:
                              Bico, my man, are you here?

A Journal of English Days

—Kensington Church Walk, St. Mary Abbots
Grey stone and dun through the mustard edges of chestnut leaves.
Inside, a funeral's going on and I back off
To sit on a wooden bench
Against a brick wall
                in the slick, unseasonable sunshine,
Trying to piece together
The way it must have been for someone in 1908
Fresh up from Italy,
A couple of books of his own poems in one hand
                          and a dead galaxy
Set to go off in crystal inside his head.
Over the stained-glass windows in front of me,
In Kensington black and white,
                Ancient Lights
Is nailed to the churchside stone,
The children trailing out of the false penumbra
                    into the sun-screed in Indian file
Then in again, shrilling, in cadence, their little song.

—I'm back for a second look,
                but someone is meditating on last week's bench
In a full lotus. Now he touches his nose
With his right forefinger, and now
With his left.
          His black shoes puddle beneath him
Like backs of mirrors he'll walk on tenderly
Over the flat-laid churchyard gravestones when he leaves.

But now he's back in position,
                              hands cupped
In his lap, thumb end touching thumb end, his eyes closed—

One of those weightless, effortless late September days
As sycamore leaves
                    tack down the unresisting air
Onto the fire-knots of late roses
Still pumping their petals of flame
                              up from the English loam,
And I suddenly recognize
The difference between the spirit and flesh
                              is finite, and slowly transgressable . . .

                                        (October)
—October everywhere out of the sunlight
Onto the China jade of the blowing fields
Of Kensington Gardens—
                        or else come down like wet lint
Over the Avon, soaking the glass.
It swivels my eyes that work me for grief and affliction
And pink my spirit, it guides my hand.

Fulke Greville lies in his stone boat in the church of St. Mary
In Warwickshire, not rippling the cold
Which clings like water drops to what was his face
On the other side of the light.

His kinsmen, Lords of the Bear and the Ragged Staff,
                              lie scattered around him,
Hermetically sealed in stone,
Who was friend to Elizabeth R and Sir Philip Sidney, ghost
In his own room now,
                  all passions heeled.

This afternoon I came up
Out of his Warwick dungeon
                    into the slow swish of the English rain,

Its bead curtain and lengths of chain
Strangely consoling after the iron artifacts
Hanging below like rib cages
                              and lungs in the torturous gloom.

The castle seemed to encircle me with its stone wings
And all of it lift
                    slightly at once, then settle back
As though the wind had died
That blows continuously under our feet
Holding up everything, then started again,
                                    and what had sunk was risen,
I don't know, at least to where it began . . .

—October's a kind time,
The rain lying like loose bandages over the ground,
The white bounty of mushrooms thrusting their flesh up,
The comforting slide of darkness
                              edging like deep water
Back through the afternoon.
The sycamore trees in Lennox Gardens crisp and spray
In the wind, our discontent,
                        like Orpheus, singing elsewhere,
Charon, in slow motion, poling his empty boat
Cross-current, over the dark water
Into the different music of London traffic,
                              the coin still clenched in his teeth
The other side of the Thames . . .

Back in the Gardens, it's tag end of a skitterish day,
October 17th, Sir Philip dead
397 years today,
I watch the stiff papers scudding across the lawn,
Leaves heaped to vindicate speedily
The offices of the end,
                        dogs nosing the moist-eared edges of things,
Noticing gradually

A larger darkness inching up through the dark
Like grass, that means to cover us all.
Across the way, the yellow moths of the window lights
Break from their blue cocoons.

—The trees stay green longer here, lacking
The clubbing frost that stuns them to glory.
                              Their leaves lie in limes and tans
Flocking the grass, vaguely pre-Cubist to me,
And blurred, without my glasses, arranged
In an almost-pattern of colors across the yard,
The same colors Cézanne once used in the same way
So often down in Provence.
                              He died there today
Seventy-seven years ago, October 22nd, the fields and houses and trees
Still these colors and pure arrangements
Oozing out of the earth, dropping out of the sky
                              in memory of him each year
Everywhere, north and south . . .

He never painted the moon.
Never romantic enough,
                    he saw what he saw in a white light.
Still, I remember it there, hanging like a doubloon
Over Puyricard, outside Aix, some fifteen years ago,
Godfrey and I in our yellow suits
                    vamping the landscape
Along the canal, first in its half, then two weeks later its full dress.
It's here now, powdering through the trees
                    as cars go by and drunks sing in the street.
The blue light from a TV swarms at the windowpanes
In one of the Dutch Georgians across the way.
He made us see differently, where the hooks fit, and the eyes go . . .
Nothing is ever finished.

127)

—Up from the basement flat at 43A,

                            up past the Greek college,
Across Walton to Ovington Gardens
Then over to Brompton Road
And across,
             left to the Oratory and right
Up under the chestnut trees to Ennismore Mews,
Up past the gardens and Prince's Gate
Across the main road and Rotten Row,
                        bicycle track
And long grass down to the Serpentine,
Ducks on the water, geese on the water, the paired swans
Imperious and the gulls
                  neat on the slick edges,
Then backtrack and a right turn
To the west, across the road and into Kensington Gardens
And out to the chestnut and beech grove
As the dogs go by
             and the Punks noodle along
In their chrome stud belts and Technicolor hair.

What breeze-bristled cities the trees are,
Their lights snatched off and on,
                  streets cluttered with leaves.
The sky is scrubbed to a delft blue
                  in the present tense,
Segueing into grey and a future pearl.

I'm stuck here, unwilling to trace my steps back,
The month running down like a love affair
                        inexorably to its close,
Sunday, October 30th, Pound's birthday ninety-eight years ago,
Everything lidded with grey, unporridgy clouds now,
Smooth as a slice of tin
              or a flat rock in the street.
Like a bouffant hairdo of steel wool,

The limbs of a leafless chestnut tree are back-combed by the wind.
The English mind, he said, the cold soup of the English mind.
At Pisa it all came back
                              in a different light
In the wind-sear and sun-sear of the death cages,
Remembering Christmases in the country, the names
Of dead friends in the Tuscan twilight
                              building and disappearing across the sky.
Cold soup, cold soup,
Longwater color of pewter,
                              late grass green neon.

—*Short Riff for John Keats on His 188th Birthday*

Hopkins thought your verse abandoned itself
To an enervating luxury,
                              a life of impressions
In fairyland, life of a dreamer,
And lacking the manly virtues of active thought.

Born on All Hallows' Eve, what other early interest
Can one assume,
                              that single, arterial drop of blood
On the clean sheet dispelling for good
                              a subsequent second,
Little black light magnet, imagination's Buddha . . .

                                                  (November)
—*A Traveler between life and death* . . .
Where is that line between sleep and sleep,
That line like a wind over water
Rippling toward shore,
                              appearing and disappearing
In wind-rise and wind-falter—
That line between rain and sleet,
                              between leaf-bronze and leaf-drop—

129)

That line where the river stops and the lake begins,
Where the black blackens
                           and light comes out of the light . . .

Stone circle at Castlerigg,
                           Cumbrian, Paleolithic chancel
Against the November mist and vault,
Mouth-mark of the invisible, air become breath
And ecclesiastical smoke . . .

Crows, like strings of black Christmas-tree lights, burn in the bare
     trees,
And silver Y moths—though soon to die—appear at dusk,

The night coming down, a dark snow
Piecemeal and hard across the moors
                           like the ashes of Paradise
3500 years ago,
                 Helvellyn and Thirlmere
Sluicing to charcoal down-valley, water and earth

And air all bleared to the same color, an indiscriminate estuary
Shoaling into the landscape, nobody here but me
Unspooling to nothingness,
                           line after line after latched, untraceable line . . .

—November pares us like green apples,
                                        circling under our skins
In long, unbroken spirals until
We are sweet flesh for the elements
                                     surprised by the wind's shear
Curling down from the north of Wales
Like Occam's edge to Steeple Aston and Oxfordshire.

"Worst time of the year," he said,
                                   "leaves everywhere
And fresh cold to shiver your very seeds.

I've burned two piles already, Saturday morning yet"—
This in the Norman churchyard,
Grey flake and flame in a hushed mound on Delia Johnson,
                                        God Knows His Own,

Lead lines in the arteries for the first time, magpies
Hustling their double notes
                        steadily, like oars in an oarlock,
Beechwoods and whitehorns, hawthorn and mountain ash
All burning down to bare ricks
Against the dropdraft of cold as winter circles and moves in . . .

—Chelsea Embankment, 5 p.m.: Whistler pastels squished
Down the fluted water, orange,
Tamarind, apricot
                        jade on the slate slip of the river,
Tug-ducks moored at the mudbanks,
Southbank light-string reflections stretched like struck and vibrating
        pipes,
The Thames rung softly
                        cross-river, and always a different note
Under the Albert Bridge, the Chelsea and out through town—
Or star-colored steps that sink
Beneath the sharkskin of the current
                                        down to the corridors
And bone-bossed gallery gates of the end.

—I keep coming back, like a tongue to a broken tooth,
Kensington Church Walk,
                        late afternoon,
Pigeons in bas-relief and frieze on the building's edge—
There is no sickness of spirit like homesickness
When what you are sick for
                        has never been seen or heard
In this world, or even remembered
                                        except as a smear of bleached light

Opening, closing beyond any alphabet's
Recall to witness and isolate . . .

November's my favorite month,
                                    the downside of autumn
And winter in first array, the sky
Constabled now and again
Over Kensington Gardens:
                              north of the Serpentine,
A pale light on the bright side of the dark,
Everything starting to glide and refract,
                                        moving just under water . . .

—Today is fire and solution, rack
                              of veins in the ruined trees,
A warm wind from the south and crows like mistletoe in the twist
And tuck of diluvial branches—

Stay out of the way and be conspicuous,
Step back and let your story, like water, go where it will,
Cut down your desires,
                        alone, as you are, on the white heart of the earth.

—The sadness of Sunday train rides in the rain,
Little gardens and back yards
Bellied up to the buffed tracks,
Their wet laundry and broken toys beside TO LET signs,
Crushed Styrofoam cups
                        small pockets of old ice turned out,

The joyless twitter of wheels
                            and couplings turning and changing,
Whole centers of villages
Scooped out and fenced in for a high-rise or a car park,
Anguish of bitten trees, slow
Bull's-eyes of raindrops in flat, colorless water pools,

And all the south of England
Under the sponge,
                    no one in sight but the yellow-slickered rail workers
Standing like patient, exotic birds
On the outskirts of Redhill, or upline from Haywards Heath,
One on one leg, as though poised for frogs,

The desolate, wax faces
Of young mothers gripping their children from side to side
In the fleshed, electric light,
                    stunned by
Something they never asked for,
Something like somebody else's life, that they've been given,

Sadness of platforms, black umbrellas
Doleful on benches, half-opened, damp,
Tedious sense
Of expectation, the clouds
Continuing on for days past our destinations . . .

                                        (December)
—Noon like cicada wings,
                    translucence remembered, half-sheets
Of light over light on the black stones
Of the crescent walk and bodices of the rhododendron,
Red eye of the whirring sun—
                    December comes out of the ground
Shedding its skin on the bare trees,
And hovers above the northern sky
Wings like new glass,
                    wings like a thousand miles of new glass—

How sweet to think that Nature is solvency,
                                        that something empirically true
Lies just under the dead leaves
That will make us anchorites in the dark

133)

Chambers of some celestial perpetuity—

                        nice to think that,

Given the bleak alternative,

Though it hasn't proved so before,

                        and won't now

No matter what things we scrape aside—

                        God is an abstract noun.

—Flashback: a late September Sunday,

                        the V & A courtyard,

Holly and I at one end,

Bronze Buddha under some falling leaves at the other:

Weightlessness of the world's skin

                        undulating like a balloon

Losing its air around us, down drifting down

Through the faint hiss of eternity

Emptying somewhere else

                        O emptying elsewhere

This afternoon, skin

That recovers me and slides me in like a hand

As I unclench and spread

                        finger by finger inside the Buddha's eye . . .

                        —London 1983

March Journal

—After the Rapture comes, and everyone goes away
Quicker than cream in a cat's mouth,
$\qquad\qquad\qquad\qquad$ all of them gone
In an endless slipknot down the sky
$\qquad\qquad\qquad\qquad$ and its pink tongue
Into the black hole of Somewhere Else,

What will we do, left with the empty spaces of our lives
Intact,
$\qquad$ the radio frequencies still unchanged,
The same houses up for sale,
Same books unread,
$\qquad\qquad\qquad$ all comfort gone and its comforting . . .

For us, the earth is a turbulent rest,
$\qquad\qquad\qquad\qquad$ a different bed
Altogether, and kinder than that—
After the first death is the second,
A little fire in the afterglow,
$\qquad\qquad\qquad\qquad$ somewhere to warm your hands.

—The clean, clear line, incised, unbleeding,
Sharp and declarative as a cut
$\qquad\qquad\qquad\qquad$ the instant before the blood wells out . . .

—*March Blues*
The insides were blue, the color of Power Putty,
When Luke dissected the dogfish,
$\qquad\qquad\qquad\qquad$ a plastic blue
In the whey
$\qquad\qquad$ sharkskin infenestrated:

135)

Its severed tailfin bobbed like a wing nut in another pan
As he explained the dye job
                              and what connected with what,
Its pursed lips skewed and pointed straight-lined at the ceiling,
The insides so blue, so blue . . .

March gets its second wind,
                              starlings high shine in the trees
As dread puts its left foot down and then the other.
Buds hold their breaths and sit tight.
The weeping cherries
                      lower their languorous necks and nibble the grass
Sprout ends that jump headfirst from the ground,
Magnolia drums blue weight
                              next door when the sun is right.

—Rhythm comes from the roots of the world,
                              rehearsed and expandable.

—After the ice storm a shower of crystal down from the trees
Shattering over the ground
                              like cut glass twirling its rainbows,
Sunlight in flushed layers under the clouds,
Twirling and disappearing into the clenched March grass.

—Structure is binary, intent on a resolution,
Its parts tight but the whole loose
                              and endlessly repetitious.

—And here we stand, caught
In the crucifixal noon
                              with its bled, attendant bells,
And nothing to answer back with.
Forsythia purrs in its burning shell,
Jonquils, like Dante's angels, appear from their blue shoots.

How can we think to know of another's desire for darkness,
That low coo like a dove's
                                insistent outside the heart's window?
How can we think to think this?
How can we sit here, crossing out line after line,
Such five-finger exercises
                        up and down, learning our scales,

And say that all quartets are eschatological
Heuristically
                when the willows swim like medusas through the trees,
Their skins beginning to blister into a thousand green welts?
How can we think to know these things,
Clouds like full suds in the sky
                                keeping away, keeping away?

—Form is finite, an undestroyable hush over all things.

A Journal of True Confessions

—Power rigs drift like lights out past the breakwater,
                                  white, and fluorescent white,
The sea moving them up and down
In the burgeoning dawn,
                    up and down,
White as they drift and flicker over the salmon run,

Engines cut, or cut back,
Trolling herring bait or flasher lures,
                              the sea moving them up and down,
The day's great hand unfolding
Its palm as the boats drift with the tide's drift:

All morning we slipped among them,
                          Ray at the boat's wheel
Maneuvering, baiting the double hooks, tying and cutting,
Getting the depth right,
                    Mark and I
Watching the rods as their almost-invisible lines

Trailed through the boat's wake,
                          waiting for each to dip:
And when it came
We set the drag and played him,
                          the salmon jumping and silver,
Then settled like quick foil in the net's green . . .

Later, ground zero, the Strait of Juan de Fuca
                                  sliding the fog out
Uncharacteristically, sunlight letting its lines down

For a last run,
                  glint from the water like flecked scales,
Everything easing away, away,

Waves, and the sea-slack, sunset,
Tide's bolt shot and turned for the night,
The dark coming in,
                  dark like the dogfish coming in
Under the island's eyelid, under and down.

                                       —15 July 1984

—Lashed to the syllable and noun,
                      the strict Armageddon of the verb,
I lolled for seventeen years
Above this bay with its antimacassars of foam
On the rocks, the white, triangular tears
                      sailboats poke through the sea's spun sheet,
Houses like wads of paper dropped in the moss clumps of the trees,
Fog in its dress whites at ease along the horizon,
Trying to get the description right.
                              If nothing else,
It showed me that what you see
                      both is and is not there,
The unseen bulking in from the edges of all things,
Changing the frame with its nothingness.

Its blue immensity taught me about subtraction,
Those luminous fingerprints
                      left by the dark, their whorls
Locked in the stations of the pilgrim sun.
It taught me to underlook.
Turkey buzzards turn in their widening spins
                            over the flint
Ridged, flake-dried ground and kelp beds,
Sway-winged and shadowless in the climbing air.
Palm trees postcard the shoreline.
Something is added as the birds disappear,
                        something quite small

And indistinct and palpable as a stain
                                    of saint light on a choir stall.
                                                —6 *August 1984*

—*I can write a simple, declarative English sentence,*
Mancini said,
                    drinking a stinger and leaning back
In his green chair above the Arno.
                                    And not many can say that,
He added, running the peppermint taste
Around on his tongue.
                    Out on the river,
Down below Prato, the sun was lowering its burned body
Into the shadows.
                    Happy birthday, Lieutenant,
He quipped, and ordered another round.

Twenty-four years ago, and dog days, indeed, Fortunatus.
Six months later
                    (flash-forward across the Aegean),
Tell Laura I Love Her, PA'ed the ship's lounge, the Captain's arm
Around my shoulders, full moonlight and Jesus
                                            everything in the sky
Was beautiful . . .
                    I ducked out and turned back down to Second Class,
His sweet invective lotioning my right ear.
And stingers that night as well, for hours out of Piraeus,
Mancini grinning like Ungaretti,
                                    And then he said, What?

The stars are fastening their big buckles
                                    and flashy night shoes,
Thunder chases its own tail down the sky,
My forty-ninth year, and all my Southern senses called to horn,
August night hanging like cobwebs around my shoulders:
How existential it all is, really,
                            the starting point always the starting point
And what's-to-come still being the What's-to-Come.

Some friends, like George, lurk in the memory like locusts,
                                        while others, flat one-sided fish
Looking up, handle themselves like sweet stuff:
                                look out for them, look out for them.
                                                —25 August 1984

—Cicadas wind up their one note to a breaking point.
The sunlight, like fine thread, opens and closes us.
The wind, its voice like grasshoppers' wings,
                                                rises and falls.
Sadness is truer than happiness.

Walking tonight through the dwarf orchard,
The fruit trees seem etched like a Dürer woodcut against the sky,
The odd fruit
                burined in bas-relief,
The moon with its one foot out of the clouds,
All twenty-one trees growing darker in a deepening dark.

When the right words are found I will take them in and be filled
through with joy.
My mouth will be precious then,
                                as your mouth is precious.
If you want to hear me, you'll have to listen again.
You'll have to listen to what the wind says,
                                whatever its next direction.
                                                —9 September 1984

—It's all such a matter of abstracts—
                                love with its mouth wide open,
Affection holding its hand out,
Impalpable to the impalpable—
No one can separate the light from the light.

They say that he comes with clouds,
The faithful witness,
                the first-begotten of the dead.

And his feet are like fine brass,
His voice the perpetual sound of many waters.

The night sky is darker than the world below the world,
The stars medieval cathedral slits from a long way.
This is the dark of the *Metamorphoses*
When sparks from the horses' hooves
                                     showed us Persephone
And the Prince's car in its slash and plunge toward Hell.

Seventy-four years ago today,
                        Dino Campana, on the way back
From his pilgrimage on foot
To the holy chill of La Verna inside the Apennines
To kiss the rock where St. Francis received the stigmata,

Stopped in a small inn at Monte Filetto
And sat on a balcony all day
                              staring out at the countryside,
The hawks circling like lost angels against the painted paradise of the
     sky,
The slope below him
                    a golden painting hung from the walnut tree:

The new line will be like the first line,
                              spacial and self-contained,
Firm to the touch
But intimate, carved, as though whispered into the ear.
                                        —*25 September 1984*

—The dragon maple is shedding its scales and wet sides,
Scuffs of cloud bump past the Blue Ridge
                                    looking for home,
Some nowhere that's somewhere for them,
The iris teeter and poke on their clubbed feet:
October settles its whole weight in a blue study.

I think of the great painters in light like this,
                                        Morandi's line
Drawn on the unredemptive air, Picasso's cut
Like a laser into the dark hard of the mystery,
Cézanne with his cross-tooth brush and hook,
And sad, immaculate Rothko,
                          whose line was no line at all,

His last light crusted and weighed down,
                                        holes within holes,
This canvas filled with an emptiness, this one half full . . .
Like the sky over Locust Avenue. Like the grass.
                                        —5 October 1984

—What disappears is what stays . . .
O'Grady stories abound.
                          Born one day later than I was, my alter ego,
He points at me constantly
Across the years
                from via dei Giubbonari in Rome, spring 1965,
Asking me where the cadence is,
Dolce vitaed and nimbus-haired,
                          where's the measure we talked about?
His finger blurs in my eye.
Outside the picture,
                the Largo looms in the bleached distance behind his back.

I look for it, Desmond, I look for it constantly
In the long, musical shape of the afternoon,
                                        in the slice of sunlight pulled
Through the bulge of the ash trees
Opening like a lanced ache in the front yard,
In the sure line the mockingbird takes
                                down from the privet hedge
And over the lawn where the early shade
Puddles like bass chords under the oak,

143)

In the tangent of 4 p.m., in the uncut grass,
                              in the tangle and tongue-tie it smooths there . . .

But our lines seem such sad notes for the most part,
Pinned like reliquaries and stopgaps
                              to the cloth effigy of some saint
Laid out in the public niche
Of a mission or monastery—
St. Xavier, hear me,
                    St. Xavier, hear my heart,
Give my life meaning, heal me and take me in,
The dust like a golden net from the daylight outside
Over everything,
          candles chewing away at the darkness with their numb teeth.
                                             —19 October 1984

—According to Freud, Leonardo da Vinci made up a wax paste
For his walks from which
                      he fashioned delicate animal figurines,
Hollow and filled with air.
When he breathed into them, they floated
Like small balloons, twisting and turning,
                                    released by the air
Like Li Po's poems downriver, downwind
To the undergrowth and the sunlight's dissembling balm.
What Freud certainly made of this
Is one thing.
          What does it mean to you,
Amber menagerie swept from his sun-struck and amber hands?

Giorgio Vasari told it first,
                    and told us this one as well:
A wine grower from Belvedere
Found an uncommon lizard and gave it to Leonardo,
Who made wings for it out of the skins
Of other lizards,
          and filled the wings with mercury

Which caused them to wave and quiver
Whenever the lizard moved.

He made eyes, a beard and two horns
In the same way, tamed it, and kept it in a large box
To terrify his friends.

His games were the pure games of children,
Asking for nothing but artifice, beauty and fear.

—20 October 1984

—Function is form, form function back here where the fruit trees
Strip to November's music,
And the black cat and the tortoiseshell cat

crouch and slink,
Crouch and slink toward something I can't see
But hear the occasional fateful rustlings of,
Where the last tomatoes seep

from their red skins through the red dirt,
And sweet woodruff holds up its smooth grey sticks
Like a room full of boys

all wanting to be excused at the same time:

The song of white lights and power boats,

the sails of August and late July devolve
To simple description in the end,
Something about a dark suture
Across the lawn,

something about the way the day snips
It open and closes it
When what-comes-out has come out

and burns hard in its vacancy,
Emerging elsewhere restructured and restrung,
Like a tall cloud that all the rain has fallen out of.

The last warm wind of summer

shines in the dogwood trees
Across the street, flamingoing berries and cupped leaves
That wait to be cracked like lice

145)

Between winter's fingernails.
                    The season rusts to these odd stains
And melodramatic stutterings
In the bare spots of the yard, in the gutter angles
Brimming with crisp leftovers,
                    and gulled blooms in the rhododendrons,
Veneer, like a hard wax, of nothing on everything.

                                        —*3 November 1984*

Night Journal

—I think of Issa, a man of few words:
The world of dew
Is the world of dew.
And yet . . .
And yet . . .

—Three words contain
                        all that we know for sure of the next life
Or the last one: Close your eyes.
Everything else is gossip,
                        false mirrors, trick windows
Flashing like Dutch glass
In the undiminishable sun.

—I write it down in visible ink,
Black words that disappear when held up to the light—
I write it down
                not to remember but to forget,
Words like thousands of pieces of shot film
                                        exposed to the sun.
I never see anything but the ground.

—Everyone wants to tell his story.
The Chinese say we live in the world of the ten thousand things,
Each of the ten thousand things
                        crying out to us
Precisely nothing,
A silence whose tune we've come to understand,
Words like birthmarks,
                        embolic sunsets drying behind the tongue.

If we were as eloquent,
If what we say could spread the good news the way that dogwood does,
Its votive candles
                        phosphorous and articulate in the green haze
Of spring, surely something would hear us.

—Even a chip of beauty
                        is beauty intractable in the mind,
Words the color of wind
Moving across the fields there
                        wind-addled and wind-sprung,
Abstracted as water glints,
The fields lion-colored and rope-colored,
As in a picture of Paradise,
                        the bodies languishing over the sky
Trailing their dark identities
That drift off and sieve away to the nothingness
Behind them
                        moving across the fields there
As words move, slowly, trailing their dark identities.

—Our words, like blown kisses, are swallowed by ghosts
Along the way,
                        their destinations bereft
In a rub of brightness unending:
How distant everything always is,
                        and yet how close,
Music starting to rise like smoke from under the trees.

—Birds sing an atonal row
                        unsyncopated
From tree to tree,
                        dew chants
Whose songs have no words
                        from tree to tree
When night puts her dark lens in,
One on this limb, two others back there.

—Words, like all things, are caught in their finitude.
They start here, they finish here
No matter how high they rise—
                    my judgment is that I know this
And never love anything hard enough
That would stamp me
                    and sink me suddenly into bliss.

A Journal of the Year of the Ox

—January,
       the dragon maple sunk in its bones,
The sky grey gouache and impediment.
Pity the poor pilgrim, the setter-forth,
Under a sweep so sure,
            pity his going up and his going down.

Each year I remember less.
This past year it's been
            the Long Island of the Holston
And all its keening wires
               in a west wind that seemed to blow constantly,
Lisping the sins of the Cherokee.

How shall we hold on, when everything bright falls away?
How shall we know what calls us
               when what's past remains what's past
And unredeemed, the crystal
And wavering coefficient of what's ahead?

Thursday, purgatorial Thursday,
The Blue Ridge etched in smoke
             through the leaded panes of the oak trees,
There, then not there,
A lone squirrel running the power line,
               neck bowed like a tiny buffalo:

The Long Island of the Holston,
                                    sacred refuge ground
Of the Cherokee Nation:
                              nothing was ever killed there.
I used to cross it twice whenever I drove to the golf course.
Nobody tells you anything.

The ghost of Dragging Canoe
                              settles like snowflakes on the limbs
Of the river bushes, a cold, white skin
That bleeds when it breaks.
                              Everyone wants to touch its hem
Now that it's fallen, everyone wants to see its face.

———————

What sifts us down through a blade-change
                                    stays hidden from us,
But sifts us the same,
Scores us and alters us utterly:
From somewhere inside and somewhere outside, it smooths us down.

———————

Here's your Spook, Indaco said,
                              sliding the imitation Sandeman's sherry figurine
Toward me along the bar, memento
And laughingstock of the 163rd,
                              stamped out by the thousands
At Nove, two hours up the road.

It's usually a ceremony, all your colleagues
And fellow officers standing absurdly about
Happy you're leaving, and you too,
                                    everyone half drunk
And hilarious in his cordovan shoes.

But not this time, Indaco wadding the paper sack up,
He and someone whose name I can't call back

letting me go for good, and glad of it:
I'd lost one document, I wore my hair long, I burned it by accident
And no one ever forgot.

Such small failures, such sleeveless oblivions
We passed through
                    trying to get our lives to fit right
In what was available from day to day,
And art,
          and then the obvious end of art, that grace

Beyond its reach
                  I'd see each night as I thumbed the Berensons
And argued with Hobart and Schneeman
                                      that what's outside
The picture is more important than what's in.
They didn't agree any more than Indaco had,

All of us hungering after righteousness
Like Paul Cézanne, we thought, in his constancy.
Or Aeneas with the golden bough
                                sweeping through Hell.
O we were luminous in our ignorance O we were true.

———————

Form comes from form, it's said:
                                nothing is ever ended,
A spilling like shook glass in the air,
Water over water,
                  flame out of flame,
Whatever we can't see, whatever we can't touch,
                                                unfixed and shining . . .

———————

And today I remember nothing.
The sky is a wrung-out, China blue
                              and hides no meanings.

The trees have a pewter tinge and hide no meanings.
All of it hustles over me like a wind
                              and reminds me of nothing.

Nobody rises out of the ground in a gold mist.
Nobody slides like an acrobat
                              out of the endless atmosphere.
Nobody touches my face
Or hand.
            Not a word is said that reminds me of anything

And O it is cold now by the fake Etruscan urn
And six miniature box bushes
                              nobody stands beside
In the real wind tightening its scarf
Around the white throats
                              of everyone who is not here.

The cold, almost solid, lies
Like snow outside
                    in the tufted spikes of the seed grass
And footprints we didn't leave
That cross the driveway and disappear up the front steps.

It's not the darkness we die of, as someone said,
                              seamless and shut tight
As water we warm up and rock in,
But cold, the cold with its quartz teeth
And fingernails
            that wears us away, wears us away

Into an afterthought.
                  Or a glint
Down there by the dwarf spruce and the squirrel run.
Or one of the absences who lips at the edge of understanding

Wherever I turn,
        as pursed and glittering as a kiss.
                            —20 January 1985

—The sunset, Mannerist clouds
                just shy of the Blue Ridge
Gainsay the age before they lose their blush
In the rising coagulation of five o'clock.
Two dark, unidentifiable birds
             swoop and climb
Out of the picture, the white-slatted, red-roofed Munch house
Gathering light as the evening begins to clot.
The trees dissolve in their plenitude
               into a dark forest
And streetlights come on to stare like praying mantises down on us.

Next morning all's inside out,
                the winter trees with their nervous systems
Snatched up and sparkless against the sky.
Light lies without desire on the black wires
And the white wires,
           the dead leaves sing like gnats,
Rising and settling back when the wind comes.
How does one deal with what is always falling away,
Returning diminished with each turn?
The grass knows, stunned in its lockjaw bed,
                   but it won't tell.
                           —30 January 1985

—We stand at the green gates,
                substitutes for the unseen
Rising like water inside our bodies,
Stand-ins against the invisible:
It's the blank sky of the page
            —not the words it's never the words—
That backgrounds our lives:
It's you always you and not your new suit

That elicits solicitude:
The unknown repeats us, and quickens our in-between.

Winter is like that—abstract,
                      flat planes and slashes,
The Blue Ridge like a worm's back
Straight ahead,
                one skewed hump and then a smooth one,
Hallelujah of tree branches and telephone poles
In front, and a house or two and a nurse:
February music,
              high notes and a thin line strung
For us to cleave to, black notes
Someone is humming we haven't been introduced to:
Like the stone inside a rock,
                the stillness of form is the center of everything,
Inalterable, always at ease.
                                        —7 February 1985

—The rain, in its white disguise,
                      has nothing to say to the wind
That carries it, whose shoulders
It slips from giving no signal, aimlessly, one drop
At a time, no word
Or gesture to what has carried it all this way for nothing.

This is the disappearance we all dreamed of when young,
Without apology, tougher than water, no word
To anyone,
              disguised as ourselves
And unrecognizable, unique
And indistinguishable from what we disappeared into.
                                        —13 February 1985

—One, one and by one we all slip into the landscape,
Under the muddy patches,
                      locked in the frozen bud

155)

Of the down-leafed rhododendron,
Or blurred in the echoing white of a rabbit's tail
Chalked on the winter's dark
                    in the back yard or the driveway.

One, one and by one we all sift to a difference
And cry out if one of our branches snaps
                    or our bark is cut.
The winter sunlight scours us,
The winter wind is our comfort and consolation.
We settle into our ruin

One, one and by one as we slip from clear rags into feathery skin
Or juice-in-the-ground, pooled
And biding its time
                    backwashed under the slick peach tree.
One, one and by one thrust up by the creek bank,
Huddled in spongy colonies,
                    longing to be listened to.

Here I am, here I am, we all say,
                    I'm back,
Rustle and wave, chatter and spring
Up to the air, the sweet air.
Hardened around the woodpecker's hole, under his down,
We all slip into the landscape, one, one and by one.
                    —*25 February 1985*

—Fever and ooze, fever and ooze:
Pronoun by pronoun, verb by irregular verb,
Winter grows great with spring: March:
                    already something has let loose
Deep in the hidden undersprings
Of the year, looking for some way out: moss sings
At the threshold, tongues wag
                    down the secret valleys and dark draws
Under the sun-stunned grass:

156)

What can't stop comes on, mewling like blood-rush in the ear,
Balancing over the sunken world:
                              fever and ooze, fever and ooze.
                                             —9 March 1985

—I used to sit on one of the benches along the Adige
In a small park upriver from S. Anastasia
                              from time to time
When I lived in Verona,
                    the Roman theater like lapped wings
On some seabird across the water
Unable to rise, half folded, half turned in the pocked air
The river spray threw up
                    on me and on it.
Catullus's seat—VALERI—was carved on top of the left-hand wing.
I used to try to imagine—delicious impossibility—
What it must have been like to be him,
                              his vowels and consonants
The color of bee wings hived in the bee-colored afternoons.
An iron-spiked and barbed-wire jut-out and overhang loomed
Just to my left.
            I always sat as close to it as I could.

I remember a woman I saw there once,
                              in March,
The daylight starting to shake its hair out like torch flames
Across the river,
                the season poised like a veiled bride,
White foot in its golden shoe
Beating the ground, full of desire, white foot at the white threshold.
She stared at the conched hillside
                         as though the season became her,
As though a threshold were opening
Somewhere inside her, no woman more beautiful than she was,
No song more insistent than the beat of that white foot,
As she stepped over,
                full of desire,

157)

Her golden shoe like a sun in the day's deep chamber.
I remember the way she looked as she stood there,
                                    that look on her face.
                                    —*27 March 1985*

—Such a hustle of blue skies from the west,
                              the pre-Columbian clouds
Brooding and looking straight down,
The white plumes of the crab-apple tree
Plunging and streaming in their invisible headgear.

April plugs in the rosebud
                  and its Tiffany limbs.
This earth is a plenitude, but it all twists into the dark,
The not no image can cut
Or color replenish.
                  Not red, not yellow, not blue.
                                    —*9 April 1985*

—Draining the Great Valley of Southwest Virginia
                              and Upper East Tennessee,
The Holston River cuts through the water gaps and the wind gaps
In the Stone Mountains and Iron Mountains
Northeast-southwest,
                  a trellis pattern of feeder streams
Like a grid from Saltville in the north
To Morristown and Jefferson City in the south
Overlaying the uplifts and folds
                              and crystalline highlands
That define and channel the main valley,
Clinch Mountain forming a western wall,
The Great Smokies and the Unakas dominant in the south.

In 1779 it took John Donelson from December till March
To go from Kingsport to Knoxville on it
By flatboat, a distance nowadays of two hours by car.

All of my childhood was spent on rivers,
The Tennessee and Hiwassee, the Little Pigeon,
The Watauga and Holston.
                              There's something about a river
No ocean can answer to:
Leonardo da Vinci,
                    in one of his notebooks,
Says that the water you touch is the last of what has passed by
And the first of what's to come.

The Cherokee called it Hogoheegee,
                                    the Holston,
From its source in Virginia down to the mouth of the French Broad.
Donelson's flotilla to Middle Tennessee
From Fort Patrick Henry
                          —one of the singular achievements
In opening the West—
Began from the Long Island of the Holston, across
The river and upwind of the fort.
It took them four months, down the Holston and Tennessee,
Up the Ohio and Cumberland,
                              to reach Nashville,
The Big Salt Lick, and the log cabins of settlement.

Intended by God's Permission, his journal said,
Through Indian ambush, death by drowning, death by fire,
Privation and frostbite,
                          their clothes much cut by bullets,
Over the thirty miles of Muscle Shoals,
Loss of the pox-carrying boat and its twenty-eight people
Which followed behind in quarantine and was cut off,
Intercepted, and all its occupants
                                butchered or taken prisoner
Their cries distinctly heard by those boats in the rear,
Passage beyond the Whirl,
                          the suckpool by Cumberland Mountain,

Slaughter of swans, slaughter of buffalo,

> *Intended by God's Permission* . . .

Imagine them standing there
> in full headdress and harness
Having to give it all up,
> another agreement in blackface,
This one the Long Island of the Holston Peace Treaty,
Ending, the first time, the Cherokee Nation.
Imagine them standing very still,
Protecting their families, hoping to hang on to their one life.
Imagine the way they must have felt
> agreeing to give away
What wasn't assignable,
The ground that everyone walked on,
> all the magic of water,
Wind in the trees, sunlight, all the magic of water.

> —16 April 1985

—April, and mirror-slide of the fatal quiet,
Butterflies in a dark confusion over the flower's clenched cheeks,
The smell of chlorophyll
> climbing like desperation across my skin:
The maple is flocked, and the sky is choked with cloud tufts
That print a black alphabet
> along the hillsides and short lawns,
Block gutturals and half thoughts
Against the oily valves opening and closing in the leaves,
Edgy, autumnal morning,
April, stretched out at ease above the garden,
> that rises and bows
To whatever it fancies:
Precious stones, the wind's cloth, Prester John or the boy-king of
    Babylon,

April,
       dank, unseasonable winter of the dead.

                                        —27 April 1985

—Visiting Emily Dickinson

We stood in the cupola for a while,
                  JT, Joe Langland and I,
And then they left and I sat
Where she'd sat, and looked through the oak tree toward the hat
     factory
And down to the river, the railroad

Still there, the streets where the caissons growled
                            with their blue meat
Still there, and Austin and Sue's still there
Next door on the other side.
And the train station at the top of the hill.
                     And I sat there and I sat there

A decade or so ago
One afternoon toward the end of winter, the oak tree
Floating its ganglia like a dark cloud
                  outside the window.
Or like a medusa hung up to dry.

And nothing came up through my feet like electric fire.
And no one appeared in a white dress
                  with white flowers
Clutched in her white, tiny hands:
No voice from nowhere said anything
                  about living and dying in 1862.

But I liked it there. I liked
The way sunlight lay like a shirtwaist over the window seat.
I liked the view down to the garden.
                  I liked the boxwood and evergreens
And the wren-like, sherry-eyed figure

I kept thinking I saw there
                    as the skies started to blossom
And a noiseless noise began to come from the orchard—
And I sat very still, and listened hard
And thought I heard it again.
                        And then there was nothing, nothing at all,

The slick bodice of sunlight
                    smoothed out on the floorboards,
The crystal I'd turned inside of
Dissembling to shine and a glaze somewhere near the windowpanes,
Voices starting to drift up from downstairs,
                      somebody calling my name . . .
                         —6 May 1985

—Ficino tells us the Absolute
Wakens the drowsy, lights the obscure,
                    revives the dead,
Gives form to the formless and finishes the incomplete.
What better good can be spoken of?
                         —9 May 1985

—In the first inch of afternoon, under the peach trees,
The constellations of sunlight
Sifting along their courses among the posed limbs,
It's hard to imagine the north wind
                    wishing us ill,
Revealing nothing at all and wishing us ill
In God's third face.
                The world is an ampersand,
And I lie in sweet clover,
                  bees like golden earrings
Dangling and locked fast to its white heads,
Watching the clouds move and the constellations of light move
Through the trees, as they both will
When the wind weathers them on their way,

When the wind weathers them to that point
                              where all things meet.
                                    —*15 May 1985*

—For two months I've wanted to write about Edgar Allan Poe,
Who lived for a year where I live now
In 1826,
              the year that Mr. Jefferson died.
He lived, appropriately enough, at 13 West Range:
One room with a fireplace and bed,
                              one table and candlestick,
A small trunk and a washstand.
There's a top hat and a black hat box on the trunk lid.
There's a grey cape on the clothes rack
                              and a bowl of mold-haired fruit
On the washstand.
              There's a mirror and cane-back chair.

Over the door, in Latin, are bronze words
About the *Magni Poetae* which I don't believe
Any more now than I used to before I lived here.
Still, there's something about the place
                              that draws me
A couple of times a week
To peer through the slab-glass door,
To knock twice with my left hand on the left doorjamb
Each time I go there,
              hoping to call the spirits up
Or just to say hello.
              He died in fear and away from home.

I went to his grave once in Baltimore,
                              a young lieutenant
Intent on intensity.
I can't remember what I thought it meant to me then,
But can remember going back to the BOQ
To sit up most of the night

163)

drinking red wine and reading a book of poems.
Here in Virginia when I visit his room and knock
Twice on the doorjamb, and look at the rump-sprung mattress,
The spirits come and my skin sings.
I still don't know why
                    but I think it's all right, and I like it.

                                        —*23 May 1985*

—Horn music starts up and stutters uncertainly
                                        out of the brown house
Across the street: a solo,
A duet, then three of them all at once, then silence,
Then up and back down the scale.
Sunday, the ninth of June, the morning
Still dull-eyed in its green kimono,
                              the loose, blown sleeves
Moving complacently in the wind.
Now there are two, then all three again
                              weaving a blurred, harmonic line
Through the oak trees and the dogwood
As the wind blows and the sheer nightgown of daylight glints.

Where was it I heard before
Those same runs and half-riffs
                        turned through a summer morning,
Come from one of the pastel buildings
Outside the window I sat in front of looking down
As I tried to practice my own scales
                              of invisible music
I thought I heard for hours on a yellow legal pad?
Verona, I think, the stiff French horn
Each weekend echoing my own false notes
                              and scrambled lines
I tried to use as decoys to coax the real things down
Out of the air they hid in and out of the pencils they hid in . . .

Silence again. For good, now,
I suspect, until next week,
                        arduous harmony,
Unalterable music our lives are measured by.
What will become of us, the Italian French horn player,
These players, me, all of us
                        trying to imitate
What we can't see and what we can't hear?
Nothing spectacular, I would guess, a life
Scored more or less by others,
                        smorzando here, *andante* there:
Only the music will stay untouched,
Moving as certainly as the wind moves,
                        invisible in the trees.
                                    —12 June 1985

—North wind flows from the mountain like water,
                                    a clear constancy
Runneling through the grapevines,
Slipping and eddying over the furrows the grasses make
Between the heaves and slackening of the vine rows,
Easing and lengthening over the trees,
                        then smooth, flat
And without sound onto the plain below.
It parts the lizard-colored beech leaves,
Nudges and slithers around
                        the winter-killed cypress
Which stand like odd animals,
Brown-furred and hung from the sky,
                        backwashes against the hillsides
And nibbles my cheeks and hands
Where I stand on the balcony letting it scour me.
Lamentation of finches,
                        harangue of the sparrow,
Nothing else moves but wind in the dog-sleep of late afternoon . . .

---

165)

Inside the self is another self like a black hole
Constantly dying, pulling parts of our lives
Always into its fluttery light,

                         anxious as Augustine
For redemption and explanation:
No birds hang in its painted and polished skies, no trees
Mark and exclaim its hill lines,

                    no grass moves, no water:

Like souls looking for bodies after some Last Judgment,
Forgotten incidents rise

                from under the stone slabs
Into its waxed air;
Grief sits like a toad with its cheeks puffed,
Immovable, motionless, its tongue like a trick whip
Picking our sorrows off, our days and our happiness;

Despair, with its three mouths full,
Dangles our good occasions, such as they are, in its grey hands,
Feeding them in,

              medieval and naked in their ecstasy;
And Death, a tiny o of blackness,
Waits like an eye for us to fall through its retina,
A minor irritation,

                so it can blink us back.

Nothing's so beautiful as the memory of it
Gathering light as glass does,
As glass does when the sundown is on it

                and darkness is still a thousand miles away.

Last night, in the second yard, salmon-smoke in the west
Back-vaulting the bats

              who plunged and swooped like wrong angels
Hooking their slipped souls in the twilight,

The quattrocento landscape
                    turning to air beneath my feet,
I sat on the stone wall as the white shirts of my son and friend
Moved through the upper yard like candles
Among the fruit trees,
                    and the high voices of children
Sifted like mist from the road below
In a game I'd never played,
                    and knew that everything was a shining,
That whatever I could see was filled with the drained light
Lapping away from me quietly,
Disappearing between the vine rows,
                    creeping back through the hills,
That anything I could feel,
                    anything I could put my hand on—
The damasked mimosa leaf,
The stone ball on the gate post, the snail shell in its still turning—
Would burst into brilliance at my touch.
But I sat still, and I touched nothing,
                    afraid that something might change
And change me beyond my knowing,
That everything I had hoped for, all I had ever wanted,
Might actually happen.
                    So I sat still and touched nothing.

———————

Six-thirty, summer evening, the swallow's hour
Over the vine rows:
                    arrowing down the valley, banking back
And sliding against the wind, they feint
And rise, invisible sustenance disappearing
Out of the air:
                    in the long, dark beams of the farmhouse,
The termites and rhinoceros beetles bore in their slow lines
Under another sky:
                    everything eats or is eaten.

———————

167)

I find myself in my own image, and am neither and both.
I come and go in myself
                              as though from room to room,
As though the smooth incarnation of some medieval spirit
Escaping my own mouth and reswallowed at leisure,
Dissembling and at my ease.
The dove drones on the hillside,
                              hidden inside the dead pine tree.
The wasp drills through the air.
I am neither, I am both.
Inside the turtle dove is the turtle dove,
                              a serious moan.
Inside the wasp we don't know, and a single drop of poison.

This part of the farmhouse was built in the fourteenth century.
Huge chains hold the central beam
                              and the wall together.
It creaks like a ship when the walls shift in the afternoon wind.

Who is it here in the night garden,
                              gown a transparent rose
Down to his ankles, great sleeves
Spreading the darkness around him wherever he steps,
Laurel corona encircling his red transparent headcap,
Pointing toward the Madonna?
Who else could it be,
                              voice like a slow rip through silk cloth
In disapproval? *Brother,* he says, pointing insistently,
A sound of voices starting to turn in the wind and then disappear as
    though
Orbiting us, *Brother, remember the way it was*
In my time: nothing has changed:
Penitents terrace the mountainside, the stars hang in their bright courses
And darkness is still the dark:
                              concentrate, listen hard,

Look to the nature of all things,
And vanished into the oncoming disappearing
Circle of voices slipstreaming through the oiled evening.

Hmmm . . . Not exactly transplendent:
                              Look to the nature of all things . . .
The clouds slide from the west to the east
Over the Berici Mountains, hiding the half of what he spoke of.
Wind is asleep in the trees,
                    weighing the shelled leaves down.
A radio comes and goes from a parked car below the hill.
What *is* it these children chant about
In their games?
              Why are their voices so like those
I thought I heard just moments ago
Centrifugal in their extantsy?
                    Concentrate, listen hard . . .
A motor scooter whines up the hill road, toward the Madonna.
                                        —9 July 1985
                                        (Cà Paruta)

—All morning the long-bellied, two-hitched drag trucks
Have ground down the mountainside
                    loaded with huge, cut stone
From two quarries being worked
Some miles up the slope. Rock-drilled and squared-off,
They make the brakes sing and the tires moan,
A music of sure contrition that troubles our ears
And shudders the farmhouse walls.
                        No one around here seems to know
Where the great loads go or what they are being used for.
But everyone suffers the music,
We all sway to the same tune
                    when the great stones pass by,
A weight that keeps us pressed to our chairs
And pushes our heads down, and slows our feet.

Volcanic originally, the Euganean Hills
Blister a tiny part,
                          upper northeast, of the Po flood plain.
Monasteries and radar stations
Relay the word from their isolate concentration,
Grouped, as they are, like bread mold
                                    and terraced like Purgatory.
Their vineyards are visible for miles,
                                cut like a gentle and green
Strip-mining curl up the steep slopes.
During the storm-sweeps out of the Alps,
From a wide distance they stand like a delicate Chinese screen
Against the immensity of the rain.

Outside my door, a cicada turns its engine on.
Above me the radar tower
Tunes its invisible music in:
                          other urgencies tell their stories
Constantly in their sleep,
Other messages plague our ears
                          under Madonna's tongue:
The twilight twists like a screw deeper into the west.

Through scenes of everyday life,
Through the dark allegory of the soul
                                into the white light of eternity,
The goddess burns in her golden car
From month to month, season to season
                                high on the walls
At the south edge of Ferrara,
Her votive and reliquary hands
Suspended and settled upon as though under glass,
Offering, giving a gentle benediction:

170)

Reality, symbol and ideal
                              tripartite and everlasting
Under the bricked, Emilian sun.

Borso, the mad uncle, giving a coin to the jester Scoccola,
Borso receiving dignitaries
                              or out hawking,
Or listening to supplications from someone down on his knees,
Or giving someone his due.
Borso d'Este, Duke of Ferrara and Modena, on a spring day
On horseback off to the hunt:
                              a dog noses a duck up from a pond,
Peasants are pruning the vines back, and grafting new ones
Delicately, as though in a dance,
Ghostly noblemen ride their horses over the archway,
A child is eating something down to the right,
                              a monkey climbs someone's leg . . .

Such a narrow, meaningful strip
                              of arrows and snakes.
Circles and purple robes, griffins and questing pilgrims:
At the tip of the lion's tail, a courtier rips
A haunch of venison with his teeth;
At the lion's head,
                              someone sits in a brushed, celestial tree.
What darkness can be objectified by this dance pose
And musician holding a dead bird
At each end of the scales?
                              What dark prayer can possibly escape
The black, cracked lips of this mendicant woman on her pooled knees?
The shadowy ribbon offers its warnings up
                              under the green eyes of heaven.

Up there, in the third realm,
                              light as though under water
Washes and folds and breaks in small waves
Over each month like sunrise:
                              triumph after triumph

Of pure Abstraction and pure Word, a paradise of white cloth
And white reflections of cloth cross-currented over the cars
With golden wheels and gold leads,

         all Concept and finery:
Love with her long hair and swans in trace,
Cybele among the Corybants,
Apollo, Medusa's blood and Attis in expiation:
All caught in the tide of light,

         all burned on the same air.

Is this the progression of our lives,

         or merely a comment on them?
Is this both the picture and what's outside the picture,
Or decoration opposing boredom
For court ladies to glance up at,

         crossing a tiled floor?
How much of what we leave do we mean to leave
And how much began as fantasy?
Questions against an idle hour as Borso looks to his hounds,
Virgo reclines on her hard bed

         under the dragon's heel,
And turreting over the green hills
And the sea, color of sunrise,

         the city floats in its marbled tear of light.

––––––––

From my balcony, the intense blue of the under-heaven,
Sapphiric and anodyne,

         backdrops Madonna's crown.
Later, an arched stretch of cloud,
Like a jet trail or a comet's trail,

         vaults over it,
A medieval ring of Paradise.
Today, it's that same blue again, blue of redemption
Against which, in the vine rows,

         the green hugs the ground hard.
Not yet, it seems to say, O not yet.

Heavy Italian afternoon: heat drives like a nail
Through the countryside,
                              everything squirms
Or lies pinned and still in its shining.
On the opposite slope, Alfredo, his long, curved scythe
Flashing and disappearing into the thick junk weeds
Between the vine stocks, moves,
                              with a breathy, whooshing sound,
Inexorably as a visitation, or some event
The afternoon's about to become the reoccasion of:
St. Catherine catching the martyr's head
                              in her white hands;
St. Catherine urging the blades on
As the wheel dazzles and turns,
Feeling the first nick like the first rung of Paradise;
St. Catherine climbing, step by step,
The shattering ladder up
                    to the small, bright hurt of the saved.
                                        —25 July 1985
                                        (Cà Paruta)

—Rilke, di Valmarana, the King of Abyssinia
And countless others once came to wash
At his memory, dipping their hands
                              into the cold waters of his name,
And signing their own
In the vellum, nineteenth-century books
The Commune of Padova provided,
                              each graced page
Now under glass in the fourteenth-century stone rooms
The poet last occupied.
We've come for the same reasons, though the great registers
No longer exist, and no one of such magnitude
Has been in evidence for some years.
                    On the cracked, restored walls,

173)

Atrocious frescoes, like those in an alcove of some trattoria,
Depict the Arcadian pursuits
He often wrote of,
                    dotted with puffy likenesses
Of the great man himself, intaglio prints of Laura
And re-creations of famous instances
In his life.
            Poems by devotees are framed and hung up
Strategically here and there.
In short, everything one would hope would not be put forth
In evidence on Petrarch's behalf.

Arquà Petrarca, the town he died in,
                              and this is,
Dangles in folds and cutbacks
Down the mountainside,
                    medieval and still undisturbed
In the backwash he retired to, and the zone remains,
Corn, vineyards and fig orchards.
The town's on the other side of the hill, and unseen,
And from the second-floor balcony,
                          southward across the Po Valley,
The prospect is just about
What he would have looked at,
                        the extra roadway and house
Gracious and unobtrusive.
I ghost from room to room and try hard
To reamalgamate everything that stays missing,
To bring together again
                      the tapestries and winter fires,
The long walks and solitude
Before the damage of history and an odd fame
Unlayered it all but the one name and a rhyme scheme.
Marconi, Victor Emmanuel II, prince
And princess have come and gone.
                        Outside, in the garden,

The hollyhocks and rose pips move quietly in the late heat.
I write my name in the dirt
                    and knock twice as we leave.

————————

Farfalla comes to my door frame,
                    enters my window,
Swivels and pirouettes, white in the white sunlight,
Farfalla and bumblebee,
Butterfly, wasp and bumblebee
                    together into the dark
Latitudes of my attic, then out
Again, all but la vespa,
The other two into the daylight, a different flower:
Vespa cruises in darkness,
                    checking the corners out,
The charred crevices fit for her habitation, black
Petals for her to light on.

————————

No clouds for four weeks, Madonna stuck
On the blue plate of the sky like sauce
                    left out overnight,
Everything flake-red and dust-peppered,
Ants slow on the doorsill,
                    flies languishing on the iron
Railing where no wind jars them.
Dead, stunned heart of summer: the blood stills to a bell pull,
The cry from the watermelon truck
                    hangs like a sheet in the dry air,
The cut grain splinters across the hillside.
All night the stalled dogs bark in our sleep.
All night the rats flutter and roll in the dark loft holes over our heads.

————————

As St. Augustine tells us, whatever is, is good,
As long as it is,

                even as it rusts and decays
In the paracletic nature of all things:

                          transplendent enough,
I'd say, for our needs, if that's what he meant
Back there in the garden in that circle of voices
Widening out of the sunset and disappearing . . .

————

Dog fire: quick singes and pops
Of lightning finger the mountainside:

                     the towers and deep dish
Are calling their children in, Madonna is calling her little ones
Out of the sky, such fine flames
To answer to and add up

                  as they all come down from the dark.
In the rings and after-chains,
In the great river of language that circles the universe,
Everything comes together,
No word is ever lost,

               no utterance ever abandoned.
They're all borne on the bodiless, glittering currents
That wash us and seek us out:

                 there is a word, one word,
For each of us, circling and holding fast
In all that cascade and light.
Said once, or said twice,

             it gathers and waits its time to come back
To its true work:

          concentrate, listen hard.

————

Enormous shadows settle across the countryside,
Scattered and misbegotten.

176)

Clouds slide from the Dolomites
                            as though let out to dry.
Sunset again: that same color of rose leaf and rose water.
The lights of another town
                            tattoo their promises
Soundlessly over the plain.
I'm back in the night garden,
                            the lower yard, between
The three dead fig trees,
Under the skeletal comb-leaves of the fanned mimosa branch,
Gazing at the Madonna,
The swallows and bats at their night work
And I at mine.
                    No scooters or trucks,
No voices of children, no alphabet in the wind:
Only this silence, the strict gospel of silence,
                                    to greet me,
Opened before me like a rare book.
I turn the first page
                    and then the next, but understand nothing,
The deepening twilight a vast vocabulary
I've never heard of.
I keep on turning, however:
                    somewhere in here, I know, is my word.
                                    —3 August 1985
                                    (Cà Paruta)

—A day licked entirely clean, the landscape resettled
Immeasurably closer, focused
And held still under the ground lens of heaven,
                                    the air
As brittle as spun glass:
One of those days the sunlight stays an inch above,
                                    or an inch inside
Whatever its tongue touches:
I can't remember my own youth,
That seam of red silt I try so anxiously to unearth:

177)

A handful of dust is a handful of dust,

                                     no matter who holds it.

Always the adverb, always the ex-Etcetera . . .

                                     —20 August 1985

—On my fiftieth birthday I awoke

In a Holiday Inn just east of Winchester, Virginia,

The companionable summer rain

                            stitching the countryside

Like bagworms inside its slick cocoon:

The memory of tomorrow is yesterday's story line:

I ate breakfast and headed south,

                        the Shenandoah

Zigzagging in its small faith

Under the Lee Highway and Interstate 81,

First on my left side, then on my right,

Sluggish and underfed,

                  the absences in the heart

Silent as sparrows in the spinning rain:

How do I want to say this?

                   My mother's mother's family

For generations has sifted down

This valley like rain out of Clarke County,

                      seeping into the red clay

Overnight and vanishing into the undergrowth

Of different lives as hard as they could.

Yesterday all of us went

             to all of the places all of them left from

One way or another,

             apple groves, scrub oaks, gravestones

With short, unmellifluous, unfamiliar names,

Cold wind out of the Blue Ridge,

And reason enough in the lowering sky for leaving

A weight so sure and so fixed . . .

And now it's my turn, same river, same hard-rock landscape

Shifting to past behind me.
                              What makes us leave what we love best?
What is it inside us that keeps erasing itself
When we need it most,
That sends us into uncertainty for its own sake
And holds us flush there
                              until we begin to love it
And have to begin again?
What is it within our own lives we decline to live
Whenever we find it,
                              making our days unendurable,
And nights almost visionless?
I still don't know yet, but I do it.

In my fiftieth year, with a bad back and a worried mind,
Going down the Lee Highway,
                              the farms and villages
Rising like fog behind me,
Between the dream and the disappearance the abiding earth
Affords us each for an instant.
                              However we choose to use it
We use it and then it's gone:
Like the glint of the Shenandoah
                              at Castleman's Ferry,
Like license plates on cars we follow and then pass by,
Like what we hold and let go,
Like this country we've all come down,
                              and where it's led us,
Like what we forgot to say, each time we forget it.
                              —25–29 August 1985

—Ashes know what burns,
                    clouds savvy which way the wind blows . . .
Full moon like a bed of coals
As autumn revs up and cuts off:
Remembering winter nights like a doused light bulb
Leaning against my skin,
                    object melting into the image

179)

Under the quickly descending stars:
Once the impasse is solved, St. Augustine says, between matter and
    spirit,
Evil is merely the absence of good:
Which makes sense, if you understand what it truly means,
Full moon the color of sand now,

                and still unretractable . . .

In a bad way,
         I don't even know what I don't know,
Time like a one-eyed jack
             whose other face I can't see
Hustling me on O hustling me on,
Dark of the moon, far side of the sun, the back half of the sky.
Time is memory, he adds:
It's all in the mind's eye,
             where everything comes to one,
Conjecture, pure spirit, the evil that matter cannot present us—
As the sentence hides in the ink,
           as cancer hides in the smoke,
As dark hides in the light,
Time hides in our pockets, not stirring, not weighing much.
                    —5 *September 1985*

—Still, they tried it again, one last time,
In 1776, the Battle of Island Flats
Outside Fort Patrick Henry
           on the Long Island of the Holston,
Dragging Canoe and Abraham
             advancing quicker than frost
With their sworn braves through the countryside.

After a small skirmish between scouts and advance guards,
Dragging Canoe brought three hundred men
Into position along a quarter-of-a-mile
Fortified line of calm frontiersmen
                                    and ended for all time
The Cherokee's mystic Nation
                        with streams of blood every way.

Never so much execution in so short a time
On the frontier.
                Our spies really deserve the greatest applause.
We took a great deal of plunder and many guns.
We have a great reason to believe
They are pouring in greatest numbers upon us
                                and beg assistance of our friends.

Exaggeration and rhetoric:
Nothing was pouring on them, of course,
                            but history and its disaffection,
Stripping the vacuum of the Cherokee:
The Battle of Island Flats
Starts the inevitable exodus,
                        Tsali and the Trail of Tears . . .
                                        —15 September 1985

—Attention is the natural prayer of the soul . . .

September, the bed we lie in between summer and autumn,
Sunday in all the windows,
                        the slow snow of daylight
Flaking the holly tree and the hedge panes
As it disappears in the odd milk teeth
The grass has bared, both lips back
                            in the cool suck of dusk.

Prayer wheels, ugly as ice, turn in our eyes:

                         verbs white, nouns white,

Adjectives white on white,

               they turn in our eyes:

Nothing is lost in my eyes in your eyes

                    nothing is lost

As the wheels whiffle and spin,

               conjunction and adverb

White in the white sky of our eyes,

                   ribbons luffing goodbye . . .

September butterflies, heavy with pollen, leaf down
In ones and pairs from the oak trees

                through the dwarf orchard

And climb the gold-dusted staves of sunlight toward the south
Like notes from a lush music

            we always almost hear

But don't quite, and stutter into the understory next door.

Night now. Silence. The flowers redeem
Nothing the season can offer up,

              stars beginning to chink fast

Overhead, west wind
Shuffling the decks of the orchard leaves.
Silence again,

       a fine ash, a night inside the night.

                             —*29 September 1985*

—The shadows of leaves on the driveway and just-cut grass,
Blurred and enlarged,

             riffle in short takes

As though stirred under water, a snicked breeze
Moving their makers cross-current and cross-grained across the pool
The daylight makes in the ash tree

             and the troubled oak.

These monochromatic early days of October
Throb like a headache just back of the eyes,
                                        a music
Of dull, identical syllables
Almost all vowels,
                    ooohing and aaahing
As though they would break out in speech and tell us something.

But nothing's to be revealed,
It seems:
            each day the shadows blur and enlarge, the rain comes and
                comes back,
A dripping of consonants,
As though it too wanted to tell us something, something
Unlike the shadows and their stray signs,

Unlike the syllable the days make
Behind the eyes, cross-current and cross-grained, and unlike
The sibilance of oak tree and ash.
                            What it wants to tell us
Is ecstasy and always,
Guttural words that hang like bats in the throat,
                                their wings closed, their eyes shut:

What it wants to tell us is damped down, slick with desire,
And unaccountable
                    to weather and its apostrophes,
Dark, sweet dark, and close to hand:
Inside its body, high on a branch, a bird
                            repeats the letters of its secret name
To everything, and everything listens hard.
                                    —4 October 1985

—Truth is the absence of falsehood,
                            beauty the absence of ugliness,
Jay like a stuffed toy in the pear tree,

Afternoon light-slant deep weight
                          diluting to aftermath on the lawn,
Jay immobile and fluffed up,
Cloud like a bass note, held and slow, now on the sunlight.
The disillusioned and twice-lapsed, the fallen-away,
Become my constituency:
                          those who would die back
To splendor and rise again
From hurt and unwillingness,
                          their own ash on their tongues,
Are those I would be among,
The called, the bruised by God, by their old ways forsaken
And startled on, the shorn and weakened.

There is no loneliness where the body is.
There is no Pyrrhic degeneration of the soul there,
Dragon maple like sunset,
                          scales fired in the noon's glare
Flaking and twisting when the wind spurts,
Sky-back a Cherokee blue,
                          scales winking and flashing.
The poem is written on glass
I look through to calibrate
                          the azimuth of sun and Blue Ridge,
Angle of rise and fall the season reconstitutes.
My name is written on glass,
The emptiness that form takes, the form of emptiness
The body can never signify,
                          yellow of ash leaves on the grass,
Three birds on the dead oak limb.
                          The heart is a spondee.
                                    —12 October 1985

—It is as though, sitting out here in the dwarf orchard,
The soul had come to rest at the edge of the body,
A vacancy, a small ache,
                          the soul had come to rest
After a long passage over the wasteland and damp season.

184)

It is as though a tree had been taken out of the landscape.
It is as though a tree had been taken out
                                    and moved to one side
And the wind blew where the tree had been
As though it had never blown there before,
                                    or that hard.

Tomorrow the rain will come with its lucid elastic threads
Binding the earth and sky.
                        Tomorrow the rain will come
And the soul will start to move again,
Retracing its passage, marking itself
                        back to the center of things.
But today, in the blanched warmth of Indian summer,
It nudges the edge of the body,
The chill luminance of its absence
                        pulsing and deep,
Extraction the landscape illuminates in the body's night.
                                    —22 October 1985

—The season steps up,
                    repeating its catechism inside the leaves.
The dogwoods spell out their beads,
Wind zithers a *Kyrie eleison* over the power lines:
Sunday, humped up in majesty,
                            the new trench for the gas main
Thrums like a healing scar
Across the street, rock-and-roll
Wah-wahs from off the roof next door to Sylvia's house
                                    just down the block:

The days peel back, maples kick in their afterburners,
We harry our sins
                and expiations around the purgatorial strip
We're subject to, eyes sewn shut,
Rocks on our backs,
                escaping smoke or rising out of the flame,

Hoping the angel's sword
                    unsullied our ashed foreheads,
Hoping the way up is not the way down,
Autumn firestorm in the trees,
                       autumn under our feet . . .
                           —*29 October 1985*

—I have no interest in anything
                    but the color of leaves,
Yellow leaves drawing the light around them
Against the mumped clouds of an early November dusk—
They draw the light like gold foil
                       around their stiff bodies
And hang like Byzantium in the Byzantine sky.

I have no interest in anything
                    but the color of blood,
Blood black as a prayer book, flushed from my own body,
China black, lapping the porcelain:
                       somewhere inside me blood
Is drawing the darkness in,
Stipple by stipple into the darker waters beneath the self.

I have no interest in anything
                    but the color of breath,
Green as the meat-haunted hum of flies,
Viridian exocrine,
              wisp of the wave-urge, jade
Calvary of the begotten sigh,
Alpha of everything, green needle and green syringe.
                         —*11 November 1985*

—"If you licked my heart, you'd die,
                    poisoned by gall and anxiousness."
I read that last night in my first dream.

In the next, the leaves fell from the trees,
                                    the stars fell from the sky
Like snowflakes, slowly and vast:
As I walked through the lightfall, my footprints like small, even voids
Behind me,
                the color of starflakes settling on everything,
Light up to my ankles, then up to my knees,
I moved effortlessly through the splendor drifting around me
Until I became a dot,
                    then grained out into light,
The voids of my footprints still sunk, hard-edged and firm, where I'd
        passed.

In my last dream, just before sunrise,
I showed slides, two slides at a time,
                                of the Resurrection, one
A painting, the other a photograph.
Much later, I showed the Five Sorrows of the Virgin,
One at a time,
            three prayers of intercession and the Assumption of St. John . . .

The subject matter is not the persona, it's the person:
"If you licked my heart, you'd die,
                            poisoned by gall and anxiousness."

Today, in mid-November's ocher afternoon light,
All's otherworldly,
                    my neighbor rolling his garbage carts to the curb,
My son repacking the tulip bulbs in their black beds:
What stays important is what we don't know and what we are not,
For nothing and nothing make nothing.
                                —20 November 1985

—All my life I've stood in desire:
                            look upon me and leave me alone,
Clear my windows and doors of flies
And let them be, taking no heed of them: I abide

187)

In darkness, it is so small and indivisible,
A full food, and more precious than time:

Better to choose for your love what you can't think,
                                                better
To love what may be gotten and held,
And step above what can be cast out and covered up:
The shorter the word, the more it serves the work of the spirit:
Tread it down fast,
                have it all whole, not broken and not undone.
                                        —28 November 1985

—Last day of November, rain
Stringy and almost solid,
                        incessantly gathering darkness around it
At one in the afternoon across
                        the Long Island of the Holston:
Up-island, steam from the coal gasification plant
Of Tennessee Eastman Corporation melds
With the cloud cover and rain cover
                                halfway up Bays Mountain—
Sycamore trees, with their mace-like and tiny pendants
And chimes, bow out toward the south sluice of the South Fork
Where I stand, a twentieth-century man on ground
Holy for over ten thousand years:
Across the river, the burial sites
                        have been bulldozed and slash-stacked
Next to Smith Equipment Company;
Behind me, the chain-linked and barbed-wire fence
Cuts under the power pylon
                        from one side of the island to the other,
Enclosing the soccer fields;
Rain is continuous as I turn
From the grey, cataracted eye
                        of a television set
Caught in a junk-jam of timber and plastic against the bank,
And walk back to the footbridge

I'd crossed the river on an hour and a half before:
Next to it, off to the left,
A rectangular block of marble, backed by slab-stone,
Had been inscribed:
                    Long Island of the Holston
Sacred Cherokee Ground Relinquished by Treaty
Jan. 7, 1806.
                    3.61 Acres Returned
To the Eastern Band of Cherokee Indians by
The City of Kingsport on July 16, 1976:
Wolf Clan, Blue Clan, Deer Clan, Paint Clan, Wild Potato Clan,
Long Hair Clan, Bird Clan:

Steam stacks, sycamores, brush harbor,
                         rain like the river falling . . .
                              —*5 December 1985*

—Late afternoon, blue of the sky blue
As a dove's neck, dove
Color of winter branches among winter branches,
Guttural whistle and up,
                    December violets crooked at my feet,
Cloud-wedge starting to slide like a detached retina
Slanting across the blue
                    inaction the dove disappears in.

Mean constellations quip and annoy
                         next night against the same sky
As I seek out, unsuccessfully,
In Luke's spyglass Halley's comet and its train of ice:
An ordered and measured affection is virtuous
In its clean cause
                    however it comes close in this life.
Nothing else moves toward us out of the stars,
                         nothing else shines.
                              —*12 December 1985*

—I am poured out like water.
Who wouldn't ask for that *lightning strike,*
                            the dog's breath on your knee
Seductive and unrehearsed,
The heart resoftened and made apt for illumination,
The body then taken up and its ghostly eyes dried?
Who wouldn't ask for that light,
                            that liquefaction and entry?

The pentimento ridgeline and bulk
Of the Blue Ridge emerge
                            behind the vanished over-paint
Of the fall leaves across the street,
Cross-hatched and hard-edged, deep blue on blue.
What is a life of contemplation worth in this world?
How far can you go if you concentrate,
                            how far down?

The afternoon shuts its doors.
The heart tightens its valves,
                            the dragon maple sunk in its bones,
The grass asleep in its wheel.
The year squeezes to this point, the cold
Hung like a lantern against the dark
                            burn of a syllable:
I roll it around on my tongue, I warm its edges . . .
                            —25 December 1985

190)

Light Journal

To speak the prime word and vanish
                              into the aneurysm
Unhealed and holding the walls open,
Trip and thump of light
                    up from the fingernails and through
The slack locks and stripped vessels
At last to the inarticulation of desire . . .

––––––––––

What did I think I meant then, Greece, 1959:
                              Beauty is in the looking for it,
The light here filtered through silk,
The water moving like breathing,
Moving in turn to the tide's turn,
                    black thread through the water weave.

Whatever it was, I still mean it.

––––––––––

Everyone stands by himself
                    on the heart of the earth,
Pierced through by a ray of sunlight:
And suddenly it's evening.

It's odd what persists
                    slip-grained in the memory,
Candescent and held fast,
Odd how for twenty-six years the someone I was once has stayed
Stopped in the columns of light
Through S. Zeno's doors,
                    trying to take the next step and break clear . . .

A Journal of One Significant Landscape

April again. Aries comes forth
                          and we are released
Into the filter veins and vast line
Under the elm and apple wood.
                          The last of the daffodils
Sulphurs the half-jade grass
                          against the arbor vitae.

Better the bodying forth,
                          better the coming back.
I listen to what the quince hums,
Its music filling my ear
                          with its flushed certitude.
Wild onion narrows the latitudes.

I pale and I acquiesce.
                          Gravity empties me
Stem by stem through its deep regalia,
Resplendent and faintly anodyne,
The green of my unbecoming
                          urging me earthward.

I long to escape through the white light in the rose root,
At ease in its clean, clear joy:
Unlike the spring flowers, I don't unfold, one petal
                                        after another, in solitude—
Happiness happens, like sainthood, in spite of ourselves.

The day dies like a small child,
                              blushed and without complaint,
Its bedcovers sliding quietly to the floor.
How still the world's room holds,
                              everything stemming its breath
In exhilaration and sadness.

———

Halfway through May and I am absolved,
A litter of leaves like half notes
                              held tight in the singing trees.
Against the board fence, the candle tips of the white pines
Gutter and burn, gutter and burn
                              on the blue apse of the sky.

How do we get said what must be said,
Seep of the honeysuckle like bad water, yellow
And slick, through the privet hedge,
                              tiger iris opening like an eye
Watching us steadily now, aware that what we see

In its disappearance and inexactitude
Is not what we think we see.
                              How does one say these things?
The sheathed beaks of the waxed magnolia
Utter their couched syllables,

Shhh of noon wind mouthing the last word.
Deep in the crevices and silk ravines of the snow rose,
Under the purple beards at the lily's throat,
                              silence stock its cocoon:
Inside, in its radiance,
                    the right answer waits to be born.

———

Truthful words are not beautiful,
                    beautiful words not truthful,
Lao-tzu says. He has a point.
Nor are good words persuasive:
The way of heaven can do no real harm,
                    and it doesn't contend.

———————

Beginning of June, clouds like medieval banderoles
Out of the sky's mouth
                    back toward the east,
Explaining the painting as Cimabue once did
In Pisa, in tempera,
                    angels sending the message out

In those days. Not now, down here
Where the peaches swell like thumbs, and the little apples and pears
Buzz like unbroken codes on the sun's wire,
                    their secret shoptalk
The outtakes we would be privy to,

But never are, no matter how hard we look at them or listen.
Still, it's here in its gilt script,
                    or there, speaking in tongues.
One of the nondescript brown-headed black birds that yawp
And scramble in and out of the trees
                    latches me with his lean eye

And tells me I'm wasting my time,
                    something I'm getting used to
In my one life with its one regret
I keep on trundling here
                    in order to alter it.
You're wasting your time, he tells me again. And I am.

———————

It is not possible to read the then in the now.
It is not possible to see the blood in the needle's eye,

195)

Sky like a sheet of carbon paper
                                    repeating our poor ills
On the other side.
                    We must be good to each other.

                        ————————

Like a developing photograph,
                            the dawn hillsides appear
Black-and-white then green then rack-over into color
Down-country along the line,
House and barn as the night blanks
                                    away into morning's fixer . . .

Like dreams awaiting their dreamers, cloud-figures step forth
Then disappear in the sky, ridgelines are cut,
                                        grass moans
Under the sun's touch and drag:
With a sigh the day explains itself, and reliefs into place . . .

Like light bulbs, the pears turn on,
                            birds plink, the cow skull spins and stares
In heaven's eye, sunshine
Cheesecloths the ground beside the peach trees.
The dragon maple shivers its dry sides . . .

I put down these memorandums of my affections,
As John Clare said,
                        memory through a secondary
Being the soul of time
                        and life the principal but its shadow,
July in its second skin glistering through the trees . . .

                        ————————

For the Heavenly Father desires that we should see,
Ruysbroeck has told us,
                        and that is why

He's ever saying to our innermost spirit one deep
Unfathomable word,
                    and nothing else . . .

———————

Thus stone upon stone,
And circle on circle I raised eternally:
So step after step
I drew back in sure ascension to Paradise,

Someone once wrote about Brunelleschi—
                              Giovanbattista Strozzi,
Vasari says—when he died
Vaulting the double dome of S. Maria del Fiore
In Florence,
          which everyone said was impossible.

Paolo Uccello, on the other hand, once drew
The four elements as animals:
                    a mole for earth,
A fish for water, a salamander for fire, and for air
A chameleon which lives on air
                    and thus will assume whatever color.

In his last days, secluded inside his house, he stayed up
All night in his study, his wife said,
                    intent on perspective.
O what a lovely thing perspective is, he'd call out.

August thrusts down its flushed face,
                    disvectored at the horizon.

———————

How is the vanishing point
                    when you look at it hard?
How does it lie in the diamond zones?

What are the colors of disappearance,
                              pink and grey,
Diamond and pink and grey?
                    How are they hard to look at?

―――――――

September's the month that moves us
                    out of our instinct:
As the master said:
                    for knowledge, add something every day,
To be wise, subtract . . .
This is the season of subtraction,

When what goes away is what stays,
                              pooled in its own grace,
When loss isn't loss, and fall
Hangs on the cusp of its one responsibility,
Tiny erasures,
              palimpsest over the pear trees.

Somewhere inside the landscape
Something reverses.
                    Leaf lines recoil, the moon switches
Her tides, dry banks begin to appear
In the long conduits
              under the skin and in the heart.

I listen to dark October just over the hill,
I listen to what the weeds exhale,
                              and the pines echo,
Elect in their rectitude:
The idea of emptiness is everything to them.
                              I smooth myself, I abide.

Chinese Journal

In 1935, the year I was born,
                    Giorgio Morandi
Penciled these bottles in by leaving them out, letting
The presence of what surrounds them increase the presence
Of what is missing,
                    keeping its distance and measure.

———————

The purple-and-white spike plants
                    stand upright and spine-laced,
As though poised to fight by keeping still.
Inside their bristly circle,
The dwarf boxwood
                    flashes its tiny shields at the sun.

———————

Under the skylight, the Pothos plant
Dangles its fourteen arms
                    into the absence of its desire.
Like a medusa in the two-ply, celadon air,
Its longing is what it grows on,
                    heart-leaves in the nothingness.

———————

To shine but not to dazzle.
Falling leaves, falling water,
                    everything comes to rest.

———

What can anyone know of the sure machine that makes all things
    work?
To find one word and use it correctly,
                       providing it is the right word,
Is more than enough:
An inch of music is an inch and a half of dust.

Night Journal II

The breath of What's-Out-There sags
Like bad weather below the branches,
                              fog-sided, Venetian,
Trailing its phonemes along the ground.
                                        It says what it has to say
Carefully, without sound, word
After word imploding into articulation
And wherewithal for the unbecome.
                              I catch its drift.

And if I could answer back,
If once I had a cloudier tongue,
                              what would I say?
I'd say what it says: nothing, with all its verities
Gone to the ground and hiding:
                              I'd say what it says now,
Dangling its language like laundry between the dark limbs,
Just hushed in its cleanliness.

The absolute night backs off.
                              Hard breezes freeze in my eyelids.
The moon, stamped horn of fool's gold,
Answers for me in the arteries of the oak trees.
I long for clear water, the silence
Of risk and deep splendor,
                              the quietness inside the solitude.
I want its drop on my lip, its cold undertaking.

XIONIA

(1990)

Silent Journal

Inaudible consonant inaudible vowel
The word continues to fall
                                    in splendor around us
Window half shadow window half moon
                              back yard like a book of snow
That holds nothing and that nothing holds
Immaculate text
              not too prescient not too true

Bicoastal Journal

Noon light on the jacaranda fans
Colorless sheen,
              and distant figures disincarnate
Every so often among the trunks.
Red beards of the eucalyptus pips.
Squall line backing and filling
              over the ocean's floor,
Waves folding and splayed flat.
Three sparrows bob at the feeder, two crows bring down rain.

Rain gone, sun perched on pine limb.
Birds bathe in an ashtray.
Ocean appalled above the kelp beds,
As though softer there.
Up here, glister of water bead,
              ants edging the ponds and lakes
Swelling the tabletop.
Here come the crows again, and the doves. Here come the gulls.

—————

The contemplative soul goes out and comes back with marvelous
    quickness—
Or bends itself, as it were,
              into a circle, Richard of St. Victor says.
Or gathers itself, as it were,
In one place and is fixed there motionless
Like birds in the sky, now to the right, now to the left . . .

There are six kinds of contemplation,
                              St. Victor adds:
Imagination, and according to imagination only;
Imagination, according to reason; reason
According to imagination;
                              reason according to reason;
Above, but not beyond, reason;
                              above reason, beyond reason.

———————

First month, third day, 32 degrees.
Overcast afternoon,
                    cloud cover moving from west to east
As slow as my imagination.
Squirrels flick through the bare branches of oak trees.
Sitting outside is like sitting under the ocean:
The white pines undulate
                         as though looked at through sea wash:
Some wind ripples by, like a current.

I'd rather be elsewhere, like water
                              hugging the undergrowth,
Uncovering rocks and small windfall
Under the laurel and maple wood.
                              I'd rather be loose fire
Licking the edges of all things but the absolute
Whose murmur retoggles me.
I'd rather be memory, touching the undersides
Of all I ever touched once in the natural world.

Saturday Morning Journal

Nature, by nature, has no answers,
                                landscape the same.
Form tends toward its own dissolution.

There is an inaccessibility in the wind,
In the wind that taps the trees
With its white cane,
                    with its white cane and fingertips;
There is a twice-remove in the light
That falls,
          that falls like stained glass to the ground:

The world has been translated into a new language
Overnight, a constellation of sighs and plain sense
I understand nothing of,
                        local objects and false weather
Out of the inborn,
As though I had asked for them, as though I had been there.

December Journal

God is not offered to the senses,
                                    St. Augustine tells us,
The artificer is not his work, but is his art:
Nothing is good if it can be better.
But all these oak trees look fine to me,
                                    this Virginia cedar
Is true to its own order
And ghosts a unity beyond its single number.
This morning's hard frost, whose force is nowhere absent, is nowhere
    present.
The undulants cleanse themselves in the riverbed,
The mud striders persevere,
                                    the exceptions provide.

I keep coming back to the visible.
                                    I keep coming back
To what it leads me into,
The hymn in the hymnal,
The object, sequence and consequence.
By being exactly what it is,
It is that other, inviolate self we yearn for,
Itself and more than itself,
                                    the word inside the word.
It is the tree and what the tree stands in for, the blank,
The far side of the last equation.

                    ———————

Black and brown of December,
                                    umber and burnt orange
Under the spoked trees, front yard

Pollocked from edge feeder to edge run,
Central Virginia beyond the ridgeline spun with a back light
Into indefinition,
                        charcoal and tan, damp green . . .

Entangled in the lust of the eye,
                        we carry this world with us wherever we go,
Even into the next one:
Abstraction, the highest form, is the highest good:
Everything's beautiful that stays in its due order,
Every existing thing can be praised
                        when compared with nothingness.

————————

The seasons roll from my tongue—
Autumn, winter, the *integer vitae* of all that's in vain,
Roll unredeemed.
                        Rain falls. The utmost
Humps out to the end of nothing's branch, crooks there like an
     inchworm,
And fingers the emptiness.
December drips through my nerves,
                        a drumming of secondary things
That spells my name right,
                        heartbeat
Of slow, steady consonants.
Trash cans weigh up with water beside the curb,
Leaves flatten themselves against the ground
                        and take cover.

How are we capable of so much love
                        for things that must fall away?
How can we utter our mild retractions and still keep
Our wasting affection for this world?
                        Augustine says
This is what we desire,

The soul itself instinctively desires it.
                              He's right, of course,
No matter how due and exacting the penance is.
The rain stops, the seasons wheel
Like stars in their bright courses:
                              the cogitation of the wise
Will bind you and take you where you will not want to go.
Mimic the juniper, have mercy.

───────

The tongue cannot live up to the heart:
Raise the eyes of your affection to its affection
And let its equivalents
                    ripen in your body.
Love what you don't understand yet, and bring it to you.

From somewhere we never see comes everything that we do see.
What is important devolves
                         from the immanence of infinitude
In whatever our hands touch—
The other world is here, just under our fingertips.

A Journal of Three Questions

Bees at the six-pointed junkweed blooms,
Ants on the move on the undersides
                                    and down the stems
Into a vast, prehensile darkness
Around the roots of the wheat grass and the violets.

Who was it first recognized the beginning of the end?
How many miles exist between the light and the dark
When light and dark are obscured?
                                    Who can distinguish them?

Bees and ants are mean creatures, their powers pervasive.

Georg Trakl Journal

Sunday, first day of summer,
The whites of my eyes extinguished
                in green and blue-green,
The white sleep of noon
Settling, a fine powder,
                under the boxweed and overgrowth.
Windless, cloudless sky.
Odor of amethyst, odor of mother-of-pearl.
Beyond the mulched beds,
The roses lie open like a tear in the earth's side.
St. Thomas, if he were here,
                would put his hand just there.

Never forget where your help comes from.
Last year, and the year before,
                the landscape spoke to me
Wherever I turned,
Chook-chook and interlude chook-chook and interlude
As I sat in the orchard,
Fricatives and labials, stops and chords
                falling like sequins inside the shadows
The jack pines laid at my feet,
Little consonants, little vowels
For me to place on my tongue,
                for me to utter and shine from.

Now silence. Now no forgiveness.
                Not even a syllable
Strays through the fevered window

Or plops like a toad in the tall grass.
                              The afternoon
Dissolves in my mouth,
The landscape dwindles and whispers like rice through my dry fingers.
Now twilight. Now the bereft bodies
Of those who have never risen from the dead glide down
Through the dwarf orchard
And waver like candle flames
                              under the peach trees and go out.

Night, and the arbor vitae, like nuns,
Bow in their solitude,
                              stars hang like tiny crosses
Above the ash trees,
Lamenting their nakedness.
                              Haloes of crystal thorns
Parachute out of the sky.
The moon, like a broken mouth,
Cloistered, in ruins, the vanished landscape,
Keep their vows, their dark patience.
Nothing says anything.
                              Nothing says nothing.

Primitive Journal

There is a heaviness behind the eyes
deep as death
And without vaccine
That sends the weight of afternoon to its earthly knees
And empties the veins of all remorse
And pity it is so strong
in its instinct and gravity.

There is a weariness in us
dark as undoing
That flakes down like a snowfall.
In April, under the apple trees
And their doilied, blanked blossoms,
It fills us beyond our knowing,
oppressive as purity.

Language Journal

Late February, five o'clock: the cantaloupe-colored light,
Light of martyrs and solitaries,
Lies like a liquid on the trees
                              as though ladled there.
Jerome,
          at large in a light like this,
Cold Mountain and Paul of Thebes
Drifting like small flames back toward the sun,
Would feel at ease
                    momentarily
In their uninterruptible avenue and dance.
The cars slide past on their golden wheels
Down Locust.
              The joggers go by and grain into radiance.

The leaves of the rhododendron
                              dangle like reliquaries,
Gilded and stained in their little piles
As though spurted upon
                          by the cleave from a saint's head,
The surface of everything
Hovering above itself in an expiation of held breath
As the body of afternoon is borne back to the hills.
Sunday, stub-end of winter,
                            baroque in its seal and dazzle,
Despair like an underpainting across the landscape,
These days we define ourselves inside,
These afternoons of last light
                              through which we all depend.

Maybe the theorists are right:
                                    everything comes from language,
The actual web of root and rain
Is just an afterimage
                    pressed on the flyleaf of a book,
This first, pale envelope of forsythia unglued
By the March heat
                    only a half-thought apostrophe
And not the flesh of experience:
Nothing means anything, the slip of phrase against phrase
Contains the real way our lives
Are graphed out and understood,
                                    the transformation of adverb
To morpheme and phoneme is all we need answer to.

But I don't think so today,
                        unless the landscape is language
Itself, which it isn't.
The water beads necklaced across the bare branch of this oak tree
Have something to say now
                        but not about syllables,
For water they are, and to water they shall return.
Out of sight, out of earshot, along the vertical axis
Of meaning,
            the music of what's real,
The plainsong of being, is happening all the while.
The verb that waits for us in the trees
                                    is reconstruct, not deconstruct:
The sound of one hand clapping is the sound of one hand clapping.

Umbria mistica . . . What I remember is how
I remember it:
                from Spello to Collepino across to Assisi
Over the humpback whole of Monte Subasio,

Bird bone and twig dry,
                    dust swirls like ghosts of penitents
Working the switchbacks and hairpins down to the sanctuary,
The cowl of mid-August heat
                    like cloth on our bodies:
Who couldn't hallucinate in such an ascetic landscape?
Seductive as pain, sharp-edged as guilt,
Its deprivations are palpable in the sunlight:
Nothing's so sweet as self-denial,
                    nothing so bountiful . . .

What is it we never can quite put our finger on
Inside the centricity of surface
                    that foregrounds and drains
The abstracts we balance our lives by?
Whatever it is, the language is only its moan.
Whatever it is, the self's trace
                    lingers along it
Much in the way that lies live in lines,
That air's in the atmosphere and wine's in this grape I pick now
From the vine beside me,
                    Perugia darkening out of sight,
Assisi darkening out of sight,
Raggio verde cutlassing down
                    as it must have done before.

                    ———————

To be of use, not to be used by,
                    the language sighs,
The landscape sighs, the wide mouth
Of March sighs at the ear of evening,
Whose eye has that look of eternity in its gaze.
To be of use,
            look of eternity in its gaze,
Not to be used by . . .
This English is not the King's English,
                    it doesn't dissemble.

If anything means nothing, nothing means anything,
Full moon in the sky
Like a golden period.
                    It doesn't dissemble.

———————

Late March, spring's loop in a deep regress,
Sunlight like polyurethane
                        on the concrete blocks
And the driveway's asphalt curve . . .
I step through the alphabet
The tree limbs shadow across the grass,
                            a dark language
Of strokes and ideograms
That spells out a different story than we are used to,
A story with no beginning and no end,
                            a little one.
I leave it and cross the street.
I think it's a happy story,
                    and not about us.

Primitive Journal II

September, the fugue of dry weather
                                    repeats itself
Cleverly through the crabgrass, cleverly through the shrubs,

Repeating itself
(Someone hums in the background
                                    under the melody)
Cleverly like a sad psalm

Over the landscape, lament
Of burned roots,
                    psaltery of the sunlight:

If faith believes, and hope and love pray,
                                            then we should pray—
For true affection in the natural world.
No wisdom can bring this grace,
                                no charity touch it.

May Journal

Notes from the provinces always start
With the weather—
                  it is no different here, the sunlight
Sweeping the high May afternoon with its golden broom,
The tulips flashing themselves
Like badges before our interrogatory eyes,
The whole floor of being
                      dustless and unencumbered,
The crystal a simile the landscape half shines through,
Image within the image, the word as world as well
As note of music,
               a touchiness along the bone.

Then they go on to talk about
                    the death of the soul
(Though not in so many words) or the death of the heart
In terms of the new season—
                    an iris, say, with its blue ear
Cocked to the pulse beat of what's-to-come.
Today's note, from Charlottesville, has nothing of that, though
Iris is in abundance
And onion and rhododendron metaphor wildly.
This is a message with no message
                    apart from its meaning,
The landscape awake in its first fire and finery.

The visible world is nothing more than a trompe l'oeil
By someone wanting a moment's peace
From the knowledge that Paradise
                  is what we live in

And not a goal to yearn for, I read once in a book
(Or something to that effect), and it sounds right to me:
That which was lost has not been found,

                                  shelter is not transcendence,
Someone has written elsewhere,
I'm sure, though I haven't found it back here in the dwarf orchard,
Peach blossoms starting to pink their wings

                                      where nothing's about to fall.

What is it in all myth

                      that brings us back from the dead?
What is it that jump-starts in verisimilitude
And ends up in ecstasy,
That takes us by both hands

                        from silence to speechlessness?
What is it that brings us out of the rock with such pain,
As though the sirens had something to say to us after all
From their clover and green shore,

                           the words of their one song
Translatable, note by note?
As though the inexpressible were made inexpressible . . .

Vesper Journal

Twilight, old friend, has come back to the lower orchard.
Two grackles waddle across the grass,
Doves moan,
           petals fall like tiny skirts
From the dogwood tree next door,
                    last things in the last light.

In this world, in this half-grain of dust,
How can there be roof room
                 or place for a human voice?
One word, in whatever language, is only one word.
And language, always, is just language.

A Journal of Southern Rivers

What lasts is what you start with.
What hast thou, O my soul, with Paradise, for instance,
Is where I began, in March 1959—

                    my question has never changed,
Always the black angel asleep on my lips,

             always
The dove's moan in the mimosa tree,
The blue faces of the twice transfigured

                closing their stone eyes.

Love for the physical world,
            a liquid glory,
Instead of a struck eternity
Painted and paralyzed

          at this end and the other,
Always the black angel asleep on my lips,

             always
The dove's moan in the mimosa tree,
The blue faces of the twice transfigured

                closing their stone eyes.

We walk with one foot in each world,

              the isness of everything
Like a rock in each shoe, the way, and along-the-way.

Overcast, south wind,
Montana early July,

           fire in the barrel stove,

Bull thistle, yarrow and red clover
Adamant on the old trail.
Two jacksnipe scurry in single file across the yard.
One calls from the marsh.

Cold, rainy Thursday.
If being is Being, as Martin Heidegger says,
There is no other question,
                              nothing to answer to,
That's worth the trouble.
In awe and astonishment we regain ourselves in this world.
There is no other.

———————

The whole moon and the whole sky are reflected
                              in a dewdrop in the grass.
The depth of the drop is the height of the moon.

———————

Everything fades away beyond the self,
                              warped or plumb.
The dry summer grass is frail as hair.
How admirable are the insects that understand the ways of heaven,
The *selva illuminata*
                    that jacklights us now and then,
The nearness of nothingness,
The single spirit that lies at the root of all things.

One August starts to resemble another,
                              so many years laid bare
Under a sky like water.
The sounds of summer are everywhere:
At fifty-two, how hard it still is
                    to face all and not shirk.
How many lives must one have,
How many chances, before the right one is played out?

How can we trust the sure, true words
                              written in blue ink?
Does the amber remember the pine?

————

September thunder lays down
                              its pre-attack barrage
From the other side of the Blue Ridge.
The clouds darken, layer by layer,
Muzzle-flash of the lightning
                              singeing their undersides.
The landscape opens itself
Inch by inch to the sparks
                              and soothing rounds of the rain.

How easily one thing comes and another passes away.
How soon we become the acolytes
Of nothing and nothing's altar
                              redeems us and makes us whole
Now for the first time,
And what we are is what we are not,
                              ecstatic and unknown.
What lasts is what you start with.

————

Whose shadows are dancing upside down in the southern rivers?
Fifty-two years have passed
                              like the turning of a palm . . .

China Journal

North wind like a fine drill
                    sky Ming porcelain for a thousand miles
The danger of what's-to-come is not in its distance
Two inches can break the heart

                                        (Great Wall)

Halfway to Chengdu; past noon.
Against the brown riprap and scree grass,
Two peach trees in blossom,
                    speechless from daybreak till now.

                                        (Jialing River)

Sky color of old steam
                    the power that moves what moves
Moves as the Buddha moves unmoving
                              great river goes eastward

                                        (Leshan)

The emperor's men are dust-red from eternity,
Quince tree pale cinnabar in the field.
Invisible as dewdrops in the afterlife, time thumbs us,
Not lightly here, but not lightly there.

                                        (Xi'an)

Local Journal

November in afterpiece,
                        transitional showdown,
Commedia dell'arte of months.
Above the morning, fast-running clouds
Scuttle and rain, then snow,
                            then break to a backdrop of Venetian blue.
Wind spills from the trees.
                      How much, thrums Expiation, half
Asleep in the wings, *how much will it all add up to?*

Always the same answer out of the clouds,
                          always the same sigh.

The void exists, and enters heaven with the infinite breath,
Pythagoras said,
                    beginning first in the numbers:
Those who have come for punishment must then be punished,
Don't dandle, don't speak in the dark.

Objects do not exist,
                    by convention sweet, by convention bitter.

Still, you could have fooled me,
                      my left hand in the juniper bush
At three in the afternoon,
My right with the pruning shears
Cutting the sticks of the rhododendron back.
                           Later,
Trailing the garbage cans to the curb,
Solace of river rock, raw rood of the power pole.

Such oleaginous evenings . . .

               Time is another country.

—————

If you don't expect the unexpected,

               you'll never find it.

A hundred mountains and not one bird,
A thousand paths and no sign:
Winter along the James River:

               a shawl of bare trees
Damasks the far bank, a boat
Knocks at its mooring post.

               No one comes forth. Nothing steps
Into the underbrush or rises out of the frame.

No wind, no shudder:

               water and sky, water and sky.

The four seasons are unforgiving,

               no news, no news:
A small reward, but I accept it.
For over a half century I've waited in vain.
Wind and cloud, sunset and dusk—

               they all know where to go.

You can't escape the attention of what you can't see.

December's the denouement,

               short steps to the solstice.
Last sun. Against the mauve hills,
Winter branches smolder, burst into flame, then die out.
At one glance, autumn is gone.
Brake lights from a stalled car shine like dog's eyes through the trees.
Heaven and earth are darkened to fine ash.

               To fine ash and a white coal.

Last Journal

Out of our own mouths we are sentenced,
                                    we who put our trust in visible things.

Soon enough we will forget the world.
                              And soon enough the world will forget us.

The breath of our lives, passing from this one to that one,
Is what the wind says, its single word
                                  being the earth's delight.

Lust of the tongue, lust of the eye,
                           out of our own mouths we are sentenced . . .

Notes

The Southern Cross

Virginia Reel is for Mark Strand.
Landscape with Seated Figure and Olive Trees: Ezra Pound at Sant'Ambrogio.
Laguna Dantesca: "She" is Picarda Donati, *Paradiso,* III.
Dog Day Vespers is for David Young.
Hawaii Dantesca: Dante and the reed of humility, *Purgatorio,* I.
Bar Giamaica, 1959–60: Ugo Mulas, Italian photographer, 1928–73.
The Southern Cross is for Mark Jarman.

The Other Side of the River

Driving to Passalacqua, 1960: Caserma Passalacqua, Headquarters SETAF (Southern European Task Force), Verona, Italy.
Homage to Cesare Pavese: "Verrà la morte e avrà i tuoi occhi," "La terra e la morte," *Il mestiere di vivere.*
Cryopexy: An operation to repair, by freezing with liquid Freon gas, a tear on the eye's retina.
T'ang Notebook: Three Hundred Poems of the T'ang Dynasty, translator(s) anonymous, Hong Kong, undated.
Arkansas Traveller: Charles F. Penzel (1840–1906).
To Giacomo Leopardi in the Sky: Giacomo Leopardi, tr. Jean-Pierre Barricelli: Las Americas Publishing Co., 1963: "L'Infinito," "La vita solitaria," "Alla sua donna," "Le ricordanze," "Il passero solitario," "Canto notturno d'un pastore errante nell'Asia," "A se stesso," "Sopra un basso rilievo antico sepolcrale," "Sopra il ritratto di una bella donna," "Il tramonto della luna."

Zone Journals

Night Journal: Teaching a Stone to Talk, Annie Dillard (Harper & Row, 1982).

A Journal of the Year of the Ox: Catullus Tibullus and Pervigilium Veneris (Harvard University
    Press MCMLXXVI); *The Penguin Book of Italian Verse* (Penguin Books, 1960); *Historical
    Sketches of the Holston Valleys* by Thomas W. Preston (The Kingsport Press, 1926); "By
    the Banks of the Holston" by Jeff Daniel Marion, *The Iron Mountain Review*, Vol. 1,
    #2 (Winter 1984); *Il Palazzo di Schifanoia* by Ranieri Varese, Grafici Editoriale s.r.i.
    (Bologna, 1983); *The Cloud of Unknowing*: An English Mystic of the 14th Century (Burns
    Oates).

Light Journal: Salvatore Quasimodo, "Ed è súbito sera."

A Journal of One Significant Landscape: Lives of the Artists by Giorgio Vasari, translated by
    George Bull (Penguin Books, 1965).

Night Journal II is for Stanley Kunitz.

Xionia

Of True Religion: St. Augustine, translated by J.H.S. Burleigh. Chicago: Henry Regnery Co.,
    1959.

Language Poetries: Edited and introduced by Douglas Messerli. New York: New Directions,
    1987.

Poems: Georg Trakl, translated by Lucia Getsi. Athens, Ohio: Mundus Artium Press, 1973.

Early Greek Philosophy: Jonathan Barnes. London/New York: Penguin Books, 1987.

Richard of St. Victor: The Mystical Ark: Grover Zinn. New York: Paulist Press, 1979.

Tian Wen, A Chinese Book of Origins: Translated by Stephen Field. New York: New Directions,
    1986.

Poesia Cinese: Translated by Giacomo Prampolini. Milano: All'insegna del pesce d'oro, 1942.

"Takushanshan": Lakota Sioux.

Printed in the United States
133067LV00004B/59/A